Myths And Legends Of All Nations

Famous Stories From The Greek, German, English, Spanish, Scandinavian, Danish, French, Russian, Bohemian, Italian And Other Sources

Translated And Edited By Logan Marshall

Red and Black Publishers, St Petersburg, Florida

Originally published 1914

Library of Congress Cataloging-in-Publication Data

Marshall, Logan.
   Myths and legends of all nations : famous stories from the Greek,
   German, English, Spanish, Scandinavian, Danish, French, Russian, Bohemian,
   Italian, and other sources / translated and edited by Logan Marshall.
        p. cm.
   Originally published: Philadelphia : J.C. Winston Co., 1914.
   ISBN 978-1-934941-27-0
 1. Mythology. 2. Legends. I. Title.
   BL312.M37 2008
   398.2--dc22

                                                        2008021853

Red and Black Publishers, PO Box 7542, St Petersburg, Florida, 33734
Contact us at: info@RedandBlackPublishers.com

            Printed and manufactured in the United States of America

Contents

Preface

The myths and legends here gathered together have appealed and will continue to appeal to every age. Nowhere in the realm of fiction are there stories to compare with those which took form centuries ago when humanity was in its childhood—stories so intimately connected with the life and history and religion of the great peoples of antiquity that they have become an integral part of our own civilization, a heritage of wealth to every child that is born into the world.

The historic basis of the tales is slight; yet who can think of the Greeks without remembering the story of Troy, or of Rome without a backward glance at Æneas, fabled founder of the race and hero of Virgil's world-famous Latin epic? Any understanding of German civilization would be incomplete without knowledge of the mythical prince Siegfried, hero of the earliest literature of the Teutonic people, finally immortalized in the nineteenth century through the musical dramas of Wagner. And so one might go on. In many ways the mythology and folklore of a country are a truer index to the life of its people than any of the pages of actual history; for through these channels the imagination and the heart speak. All the chronicles of rulers and governing bodies are as dust in comparison.

The imagination of the ancients had few if any bounds, and even Athens in the height of her intellectual glory accepted the fabulous tales of gods and half-gods. Today we read and wonder. But the child, who in his brief lifetime must live over in part at least the history of the whole of humanity, delights in the myths and legends which made his ancestors admire or tremble. They are naturally not so real to him as they were to his forefathers; yet they open up a rich and gorgeous wonderland, without excursions into which every child must grow up the poorer in mind and spirit.

To the children of America, wherever they may be, this book is dedicated. It is sure to bring enjoyment, because its stories have stood the test of time.

Prometheus, The Friend Of Man

Many, many centuries ago there lived two brothers, Prometheus or Forethought, and Epimetheus or Afterthought. They were the sons of those Titans who had fought against Jupiter and been sent in chains to the great prison-house of the lower world, but for some reason had escaped punishment.

Prometheus, however, did not care for idle life among the gods on Mount Olympus. Instead he preferred to spend his time on the earth, helping men to find easier and better ways of living. For the children of earth were not happy as they had been in the golden days when Saturn ruled. Indeed, they were very poor and wretched and cold, without fire, without food, and with no shelter but miserable caves.

"With fire they could at least warm their bodies and cook their food," Prometheus thought, "and later they could make tools and build houses for themselves and enjoy some of the comforts of the gods."

So Prometheus went to Jupiter and asked that he might be permitted to carry fire to the earth. But Jupiter shook his head in wrath.

"Fire, indeed!" he exclaimed. "If men had fire they would soon be as strong and wise as we who dwell on Olympus. Never will I give my consent."

Prometheus made no reply, but he didn't give up his idea of helping men. "Some other way must be found," he thought.

Then, one day, as he was walking among some reeds he broke off one, and seeing that its hollow stalk was filled with a dry, soft pith, exclaimed:

"At last! In this I can carry fire, and the children of men shall have the great gift in spite of Jupiter."

Immediately, taking a long stalk in his hands, he set out for the dwelling of the sun in the far east. He reached there in the early morning, just as Apollo's chariot was about to begin its journey across the sky. Lighting his reed, he hurried back, carefully guarding the precious spark that was hidden in the hollow stalk.

Then he showed men how to build fires for themselves, and it was not long before they began to do all the wonderful things of which Prometheus had dreamed. They learned to cook and to domesticate animals and to till the fields and to mine precious metals and melt them into tools and weapons. And they came out of their dark and gloomy caves and built for themselves beautiful houses of wood and stone. And instead of being sad and unhappy they began to laugh and sing. "Behold, the Age of Gold has come again," they said.

But Jupiter was not so happy. He saw that men were gaining daily greater power, and their very prosperity made him angry.

"That young Titan!" he cried out, when he heard what Prometheus had done. "I will punish him."

But before punishing Prometheus he decided to vex the children of men. So he gave a lump of clay to his blacksmith, Vulcan, and told him to mold it in the form of a woman. When the work was done he carried it to Olympus.

Jupiter called the other gods together, bidding them give her each a gift. One bestowed upon her beauty, another, kindness, another, skill, another, curiosity, and so on. Jupiter himself gave her the gift of life, and they named her Pandora, which means "all-gifted."

Then Mercury, the messenger of the gods, took Pandora and led her down the mountain side to the place where Prometheus and his brother were living.

"Epimetheus, here is a beautiful woman that Jupiter has sent to be your wife," he said.

Epimetheus was delighted and soon loved Pandora very deeply, because of her beauty and her goodness.

Now Pandora had brought with her as a gift from Jupiter a golden casket. Athena had warned her never to open the box, but she could not help wondering and wondering what it contained. Perhaps it held beautiful jewels. Why should they go to waste?

At last she could not contain her curiosity any longer. She opened the box just a little to take a peep inside. Immediately there was a buzzing, whirring sound, and before she could snap down the lid ten thousand ugly little creatures had jumped out. They were diseases and troubles, and very glad they were to be free.

All over the earth they flew, entering into every household, and carrying sorrow and distress wherever they went.

How Jupiter must have laughed when he saw the result of Pandora's curiosity!

Soon after this the god decided that it was time to punish Prometheus. He called Strength and Force and bade them seize the Titan and carry him to the highest peak of the Caucasus Mountains. Then he sent Vulcan to bind him with iron chains, making arms and feet fast to the rocks. Vulcan was sorry for Prometheus, but dared not disobey.

So the friend of man lay, miserably bound, naked to the winds, while the storms beat about him and an eagle tore at his liver with its cruel talons. But Prometheus did not utter a groan in spite of all his sufferings. Year after year he lay in agony, and yet he would not complain, beg for mercy or repent of what he had done. Men were sorry for him, but could do nothing.

Then one day a beautiful white cow passed over the mountain, and stopped to look at Prometheus with sad eyes.

"I know you," Prometheus said. "You are Io, once a fair and happy maiden dwelling in Argos, doomed by Jupiter and his jealous queen to wander over the earth in this guise. Go southward and then west until you come to the great river Nile.

There you shall again become a maiden, fairer than ever before, and shall marry the king of that country. And from your race shall spring the hero who will break my chains and set me free."

Centuries passed and then a great hero, Hercules, came to the Caucasus Mountains. He climbed the rugged peak, slew the fierce eagle, and with mighty blows broke the chains that bound the friend of man.

The Labors Of Hercules

Before the birth of Hercules Jupiter had explained in the council of the gods that the first descendant of Perseus should be the ruler of all the others of his race. This honor was intended for the son of Perseus and Alcmene; but Juno was jealous and brought it about that Eurystheus, who was also a descendant of Perseus, should be born before Theseus. So Eurystheus became king in Mycene, and the later-born Hercules remained inferior to him.

Now Eurystheus watched with anxiety the rising fame of his young relative, and called his subject to him, demanding that he carry through certain great tasks or labors. When Hercules did not immediately obey, Jupiter himself sent word to him that he should fulfill his service to the King of Greece.

Nevertheless the hero son of a god could not make up his mind easily to render service to a mere mortal. So he traveled to Delphi and questioned the oracle as to what he should do. This was the answer:

The overlordship of Eurystheus will be qualified on condition that Hercules perform ten labors that Eurystheus shall assign him. When this is done, Hercules shall be numbered among the immortal gods.

Hereupon Hercules fell into deep trouble. To serve a man of less importance than himself hurt his dignity and self-esteem; but Jupiter would not listen to his complaints.

The First Labor

The first labor that Eurystheus assigned to Hercules was to bring him the skin of the Nemean lion. This monster dwelt on the mountain of Peloponnesus, in the forest between Kleona and Nemea, and could be wounded by no weapons made of man. Some said he was the son of the giant Typhon and the snake Echidna; others that he had dropped down from the moon to the earth.

Hercules set out on his journey and came to Kleona, where a poor laborer, Molorchus, received him hospitably. He met the latter just as he was about to offer a sacrifice to Jupiter.

"Good man," said Hercules, "let the animal live thirty days longer; then, if I return, offer it to Jupiter, my deliverer, and if I do not return, offer it as a funeral sacrifice to me, the hero who has attained immortality."

So Hercules continued on his way, his quiver of arrows over his shoulder, his bow in one hand, and in the other a club made from the trunk of a wild olive tree which he had passed on Mount Helicon and pulled up by the roots. When he at last entered the Nemean wood, he looked carefully in every direction in order that he might catch sight of the monster lion before the lion should see him. It was mid-day, and nowhere could he discover any trace of the lion or any path that seemed to lead to his lair. He met no man in the field or in the forest: fear held them all shut up in their distant dwellings. The whole afternoon he wandered through the thick undergrowth, determined to test his strength just as soon as he should encounter the lion.

At last, toward evening, the monster came through the forest, returning from his trap in a deep fissure of the earth.

He was saturated with blood: head, mane and breast were reeking, and his great tongue was licking his jaws. The hero, who saw him coming long before he was near, took refuge in a thicket and waited until the lion approached; then with his arrow he shot him in the side. But the shot did not pierce his flesh; instead it flew back as if it had struck stone, and fell on the mossy earth.

Then the animal raised his bloody head; looked around in every direction, and in fierce anger showed his ugly teeth. Raising his head, he exposed his heart, and immediately Hercules let fly another arrow, hoping to pierce him through the lungs. Again the arrow did not enter the flesh, but fell at the feet of the monster.

Hercules took a third arrow, while the lion, casting his eyes to the side, watched him. His whole neck swelled with anger; he roared, and his back was bent like a bow. He sprang toward his enemy; but Hercules threw the arrow and cast off the lion skin in which he was clothed with the left hand, while with the right he swung his club over the head of the beast and gave him such a blow on the neck that, all ready to spring as the lion was, he fell back, and came to a stand on trembling legs, with shaking head. Before he could take another breath, Hercules was upon him.

Throwing down his bow and quiver, that he might be entirely unencumbered, he approached the animal from behind, threw his arm around his neck and strangled him. Then for a long time he sought in vain to strip the fallen animal of his hide. It yielded to no weapon or no stone. At last the idea occurred to him of tearing it with the animal's own claws, and this method immediately succeeded.

Later he prepared for himself a coat of mail out of the lion's skin, and from the neck, a new helmet; but for the present he was content to don his own costume and weapons, and with the lion's skin over his arm took his way back to Tirynth.

The Second Labor
The second labor consisted in destroying a hydra. This monster dwelt in the swamp of Lerna, but came occasionally over the country, destroying herds and laying waste the fields.

The hydra was an enormous creature—a serpent with nine heads, of which eight were mortal and one immortal.

Hercules set out with high courage for this fight. He mounted his chariot, and his beloved nephew Iolaus, the son of his stepbrother Iphicles, who for a long time had been his inseparable companion, sat by his side, guiding the horses; and so they sped toward Lerna.

At last the hydra was visible on a hill by the springs of Amymone, where its lair was found. Here Iolaus left the horses stand. Hercules leaped from the chariot and sought with burning arrows to drive the many-headed serpent from its hiding place. It came forth hissing, its nine heads raised and swaying like the branches of a tree in a storm.

Undismayed, Hercules approached it, seized it, and held it fast. But the snake wrapped itself around one of his feet. Then he began with his sword to cut off its heads. But this looked like an endless task, for no sooner had he cut off one head than two grew in its place. At the same time an enormous crab came to the help of the hydra and began biting the hero's foot. Killing this with his club, he called to Iolaus for help.

The latter had lighted a torch, set fire to a portion of the nearby wood, and with brands therefrom touched the serpent's newly growing heads and prevented them from living. In this way the hero was at last master of the situation and was able to cut off even the head of the hydra that could not be killed. This he buried deep in the ground and rolled a heavy stone over the place. The body of the hydra he cut into half, dipping his arrows in the blood, which was poisonous.

From that time the wounds made by the arrows of Hercules were fatal.

The Third Labor
The third demand of Eurystheus was that Hercules bring to him alive the hind Cerynitis. This was a noble animal, with horns of gold and feet of iron. She lived on a hill in Arcadia, and was one of the five hinds which the goddess Diana had caught on her first hunt. This one, of all the five, was permitted to run

loose again in the woods, for it was decreed by fate that Hercules should one day hunt her.

For a whole year Hercules pursued her; came at last to the river Ladon; and there captured the hind, not far from the city Oenon, on the mountains of Diana. But he knew of no way of becoming master of the animal without wounding her, so he lamed her with an arrow and then carried her over his shoulder through Arcadia.

Here he met Diana herself with Apollo, who scolded him for wishing to kill the animal that she had held sacred, and was about to take it from him.

"Impiety did not move me, great goddess," said Hercules in his own defense, "but only the direst necessity. How otherwise could I hold my own against Eurystheus?"

And thus he softened the anger of the goddess and brought the animal to Mycene.

The Fourth Labor

Then Hercules set out on his fourth undertaking. It consisted in bringing alive to Mycene a boar which, likewise sacred to Diana, was laying waste the country around the mountain of Erymanthus.

On his wanderings in search of this adventure he came to the dwelling of Pholus, the son of Silenus. Like all Centaurs, Pholus was half man and half horse. He received his guest with hospitality and set before him broiled meat, while he himself ate raw. But Hercules, not satisfied with this, wished also to have something good to drink.

"Dear guest," said Pholus, "there is a cask in my cellar; but it belongs to all the Centaurs jointly, and I hesitate to open it because I know how little they welcome guests."

"Open it with good courage," answered Hercules, "I promise to defend you against all displeasure."

As it happened, the cask of wine had been given to the Centaurs by Bacchus, the god of wine, with the command that they should not open it until, after four centuries, Hercules should appear in their midst.

Pholus went to the cellar and opened the wonderful cask. But scarcely had he done so when the Centaurs caught the perfume of the rare old wine, and, armed with stones and pine clubs, surrounded the cave of Pholus. The first who tried to force their way in Hercules drove back with brands he seized from the fire. The rest he pursued with bow and arrow, driving them back to Malea, where lived the good Centaur, Chiron, Hercules' old friend. To him his brother Centaurs had fled for protection.

But Hercules still continued shooting, and sent an arrow through the arm of an old Centaur, which unhappily went quite through and fell on Chiron's knee, piercing the flesh. Then for the first time Hercules recognized his friend of former days, ran to him in great distress, pulled out the arrow, and laid healing ointment on the wound, as the wise Chiron himself had taught him. But the wound, filled with the poison of the hydra, could not be healed; so the centaur was carried into his cave. There he wished to die in the arms of his friend. Vain wish! The poor Centaur had forgotten that he was immortal, and though wounded would not die.

Then Hercules with many tears bade farewell to his old teacher and promised to send to him, no matter at what price, the great deliverer, Death. And we know that he kept his word.

When Hercules from the pursuit of the other Centaurs returned to the dwelling of Pholus he found him also dead. He had drawn the deadly arrow from the lifeless body of one Centaur, and while he was wondering how so small a thing could do such great damage, the poisoned arrow slipped through his fingers and pierced his foot, killing him instantly. Hercules was very sad, and buried his body reverently beneath the mountain, which from that day was called Pholoë.

Then Hercules continued his hunt for the boar, drove him with cries out of the thick of the woods, pursued him into a deep snow field, bound the exhausted animal, and brought him, as he had been commanded, alive to Mycene.

The Fifth Labor

Thereupon King Eurystheus sent him upon the fifth labor, which was one little worthy of a hero. It was to clean the stables of Augeas in a single day.

Augeas was king in Elis and had great herds of cattle. These herds were kept, according to the custom, in a great inclosure before the palace. Three thousand cattle were housed there, and as the stables had not been cleaned for many years, so much manure had accumulated that it seemed an insult to ask Hercules to clean them in one day.

When the hero stepped before King Augeas and without telling him anything of the demands of Eurystheus, pledged himself to the task, the latter measured the noble form in the lion-skin and could hardly refrain from laughing when he thought of so worthy a warrior undertaking so menial a work. But he said to himself: "Necessity has driven many a brave man; perhaps this one wishes to enrich himself through me. That will help him little. I can promise him a large reward if he cleans out the stables, for he can in one day clear little enough." Then he spoke confidently:

"Listen, O stranger. If you clean all of my stables in one day, I will give over to you the tenth part of all my possessions in cattle."

Hercules accepted the offer, and the king expected to see him begin to shovel. But Hercules, after he had called the son of Augeas to witness the agreement, tore the foundations away from one side of the stables; directed to it by means of a canal the streams of Alpheus and Peneus that flowed near by; and let the waters carry away the filth through another opening. So he accomplished the menial work without stooping to anything unworthy of an immortal.

When Augeas learned that this work had been done in the service of Eurystheus, he refused the reward and said that he had not promised it; but he declared himself ready to have the question settled in court. When the judges were assembled, Phyleus, commanded by Hercules to appear, testified against his father, and explained how he had agreed to offer Hercules a reward. Augeas did not wait for the decision; he grew angry and commanded his son as well as the stranger to leave his kingdom instantly.

The Sixth Labor

Hercules now returned with new adventures to Eurystheus; but the latter would not give him credit for the task because Hercules had demanded a reward for his labor. He sent the hero forth upon a sixth adventure, commanding him to drive away the Stymphalides. These were monster birds of prey, as large as cranes, with iron feathers, beaks and claws. They lived on the banks of Lake Stymphalus in Arcadia, and had the power of using their feathers as arrows and piercing with their beaks even bronze coats of mail. Thus they brought destruction to both animals and men in all the surrounding country.

After a short journey Hercules, accustomed to wandering, arrived at the lake, which was thickly shaded by a wood. Into this wood a great flock of the birds had flown for fear of being robbed by wolves. The hero stood undecided when he saw the frightful crowd, not knowing how he could become master over so many enemies. Then he felt a light touch on his shoulder, and glancing behind him saw the tall figure of the goddess Minerva, who gave into his hands two mighty brass rattles made by Vulcan. Telling him to use these to drive away the Stymphalides, she disappeared.

Hercules mounted a hill near the lake, and began frightening the birds by the noise of the rattles. The Stymphalides could not endure the awful noise and flew, terrified, out of the forest. Then Hercules seized his bow and sent arrow after arrow in pursuit of them, shooting many as they flew. Those who were not killed left the lake and never returned.

The Seventh Labor

King Minos of Crete had promised Neptune (Poseidon), god of the sea, to offer to him whatever animal should first come up out of the water, for he declared he had no animal that was worthy for so high a sacrifice. Therefore the god caused a very beautiful ox to rise out of the sea. But the king was so taken with the noble appearance of the animal that he secretly placed it among his own herds and offered another to Neptune. Angered by this, the god had caused the animal to become mad, and it was bringing great destruction to the island of Crete. To capture this animal, master it, and bring it before Eurystheus, was the seventh labor of Hercules.

When the hero came to Crete and with this intention stepped before Minos, the king was not a little pleased over the prospect of ridding the island of the bull, and he himself helped Hercules to capture the raging animal. Hercules approached the dreadful monster without fear, and so thoroughly did he master him that he rode home on the animal the whole way to the sea.

With this work Eurystheus was pleased, and after he had regarded the animal for a time with pleasure, set it free. No longer under Hercules' management, the ox became wild again, wandered through all Laconia and Arcadia, crossed over the isthmus to Marathon in Attica and devastated the country there as formerly on the island of Crete. Later it was given to the hero Theseus to become master over him.

The Eighth Labor

The eighth labor of Hercules was to bring the mares of the Thracian Diomede to Mycene. Diomede was a son of Mars and ruler of the Bistonians, a very warlike people. He had mares so wild and strong that they had to be fastened with iron chains. Their fodder was chiefly hay; but strangers who had the misfortune to come into the city were thrown before them, their flesh serving the animals as food.

When Hercules arrived the first thing he did was to seize the inhuman king himself and after he had overpowered the keepers, throw him before his own mares. With this food the animals were satisfied and Hercules was able to drive them to the sea.

But the Bistonians followed him with weapons, and Hercules was forced to turn and fight them. He gave the horses into the keeping of his beloved companion Abderus, the son of

Mercury, and while Hercules was away the animals grew hungry again and devoured their keeper.

Hercules, returning, was greatly grieved over this loss, and later founded a city in honor of Abderus, naming it after his lost friend. For the present he was content to master the mares and drive them without further mishap to Eurystheus.

The latter consecrated the horses to Juno. Their descendants were very powerful, and the great king Alexander of Macedonia rode one of them.

The Ninth Labor

Returning from a long journey, the hero undertook an expedition against the Amazons in order to finish the ninth adventure and bring to King Eurystheus the sword belt of the Amazon Hippolyta.

The Amazons inhabited the region of the river Thermodon and were a race of strong women who followed the occupations of men. From their children they selected only such as were girls. United in an army, they waged great wars. Their queen, Hippolyta, wore, as a sign of her leadership, a girdle which the goddess of war had given her as a present.

Hercules gathered his warrior companions together into a ship, sailed after many adventures into the Black Sea and at last into the mouth of the river Thermodon, and the harbor of the Amazon city Themiscira. Here the queen of the Amazons met him.

The lordly appearance of the hero flattered her pride, and when she heard the object of his visit, she promised him the belt. But Juno, the relentless enemy of Hercules, assuming the form of an Amazon, mingled among the others and spread the news that a stranger was about to lead away their queen. Then the Amazons fought with the warriors of Hercules, and the best fighters of them attacked the hero and gave him a hard battle.

The first who began fighting with him was called, because of her swiftness, Aëlla, or Bride of the Wind; but she found in Hercules a swifter opponent, was forced to yield and was in her swift flight overtaken by him and vanquished. A second fell at the first attack; then Prothoë, the third, who had come off victor in seven duels, also fell. Hercules laid low eight others, among them three hunter companions of Diana, who, although formerly always certain with their weapons, today failed in their aim, and vainly covering themselves with their shields fell before the arrows of the hero. Even Alkippe fell, who had sworn to live her whole life unmarried: the vow she kept, but not her life.

After even Melanippe, the brave leader of the Amazons, was made captive, all the rest took to wild flight, and Hippolyta the queen handed over the sword belt which she had promised even before the fight. Hercules took it as ransom and set Melanippe free.

The Tenth Labor

When the hero laid the sword belt of Queen Hippolyta at the feet of Eurystheus, the latter gave him no rest, but sent him out immediately to procure the cattle of the giant Geryone. The latter dwelt on an island in the midst of the sea, and possessed a herd of beautiful red-brown cattle, which were guarded by another giant and a two-headed dog.

Geryone himself was enormous, had three bodies, three heads, six arms and six feet. No son of earth had ever measured his strength against him, and Hercules realized exactly how many preparations were necessary for this heavy undertaking. As everybody knew, Geryone's father, who bore the name "Gold-Sword" because of his riches, was king of all Iberia (Spain). Besides Geryone he had three brave giant sons who fought for him; and each son had a mighty army of soldiers under his command. For these very reasons had Eurystheus given the task to Hercules, for he hoped that his hated existence would at last be ended in a war in such a country. Yet Hercules set out on this undertaking no more dismayed than on any previous expedition.

He gathered together his army on the island of Crete, which he had freed from wild animals, and landed first in Libya. Here he met the giant Antaeus, whose strength was renewed as often as he touched the earth. He also freed Libya of birds of prey; for he hated wild animals and wicked men because he saw in all of them the image of the overbearing and unjust lord whom he so long had served.

After long wandering through desert country he came at last to a fruitful land, through which great streams flowed. Here he founded a city of vast size, which he named Hecatompylos (City of a Hundred Gates). Then at last he reached the Atlantic Ocean and planted the two mighty pillars which bear his name.

The sun burned so fiercely that Hercules could bear it no longer; he raised his eyes to heaven and with raised bow threatened the sun-god. Apollo wondered at his courage and lent him for his further journeys the bark in which he himself was accustomed to lie from sunset to sunrise. In this Hercules sailed to Iberia.

Here he found the three sons of Gold-Sword with three great armies camping near each other; but he killed all the leaders and plundered the land. Then he sailed to the island Erythia, where Geryone dwelt with his herds.

As soon as the two-headed dog knew of his approach he sprang toward him; but Hercules struck him with his club and killed him. He killed also the giant herdsman who came to the help of the dog. Then he hurried away with the cattle.

But Geryone overtook him and there was a fierce struggle. Juno herself offered to assist the giant; but Hercules shot her with an arrow deep in the heart, and the goddess, wounded, fled. Even the threefold body of the giant which ran together in the region of the stomach, felt the might of the deadly arrows and was forced to yield.

With glorious adventures Hercules continued his way home, driving the cattle across country through Iberia and Italy. At Rhegium in lower Italy one of his oxen got away and swam across the strait to Sicily. Immediately Hercules drove the other cattle into the water and swam, holding one by the horns, to Sicily. Then the hero pursued his way without misfortune through Italy, Illyria and Thrace to Greece.

Hercules had now accomplished ten labors; but Eurystheus was still unsatisfied and there were two more tasks to be undertaken.

The Eleventh Labor

At the celebration of the marriage of Jupiter and Juno, when all the gods were bringing their wedding gifts to the happy pair, Mother Earth did not wish to be left out. So she caused to spring forth on the western borders of the great world-sea a many-branched tree full of golden apples. Four maidens called the Hesperides, daughters of Night, were the guardians of this sacred garden, and with them watched the hundred-headed dragon, Ladon, whose father was Phorkys, the parent of many monsters. Sleep came never to the eyes of this dragon and a fearful hissing sound warned one of his presence, for each of his hundred throats had a different voice. From this monster, so was the command of Eurystheus, should Hercules seize the golden apples.

The hero set out on his long and adventurous journey and placed himself in the hands of blind chance, for he did not know where the Hesperides dwelt.

He went first to Thessaly, where dwelt the giant Termerus, who with his skull knocked to death every traveler that he met; but on the mighty cranium of Hercules the head of the giant himself was split open.

Farther on the hero came upon another monster in his way — Cycnus, the son of Mars and Pyrene. He, when asked concerning the garden of the Hesperides, instead of answering, challenged the wanderer to a duel, and was beaten by Hercules. Then appeared Mars, the god of war, himself, to avenge the death of his son; and Hercules was forced to fight with him. But Jupiter did not wish that his sons should shed blood, and sent his lightning bolt to separate the two.

Then Hercules continued his way through Illyria, hastened over the river Eridanus, and came to the nymphs of Jupiter and Themis, who dwelt on the banks of the stream. To these Hercules put his question.

"Go to the old river god Nereus," was their answer. "He is a seer and knows all things. Surprise him while he sleeps and bind him; then he will be forced to tell you the right way."

Hercules followed this advice and became master of the river god, although the latter, according to his custom, assumed many different forms. Hercules would not let him go until he had learned in what locality he could find the golden apples of the Hesperides.

Informed of this, he went on his way toward Libya and Egypt. Over the latter land ruled Busiris, the son of Neptune and Lysianassa. To him during the period of a nine-year famine a prophet had borne the oracular message that the land would again bear fruit if a stranger were sacrificed once a year to Jupiter. In gratitude Busiris made a beginning with the priest himself. Later he found great pleasure in the custom and killed all strangers who came to Egypt. So Hercules was seized and placed on the altar of Jupiter. But he broke the chains which bound him, and killed Busiris and his son and the priestly herald.

With many adventures the hero continued his way, set free, as has been told elsewhere, Prometheus, the Titan, who was bound to the Caucasus Mountains, and came at last to the place where Atlas stood carrying the weight of the heavens on his shoulders. Near him grew the tree which bore the golden apples of the Hesperides.

Prometheus had advised the hero not to attempt himself to make the robbery of the golden fruit, but to send Atlas on the errand. The giant offered to do this if Hercules would support the heavens while he went. This Hercules consented to do, and Atlas set out. He put to sleep the dragon who lived beneath the tree and killed him. Then with a trick he got the better of the keepers, and returned happily to Hercules with the three apples which he had plucked.

"But," he said, "I have now found out how it feels to be relieved of the heavy burden of the heavens. I will not carry them any longer." Then he threw the apples down at the feet of the hero, and left him standing with the unaccustomed, awful weight upon his shoulders.

Hercules had to think of a trick in order to get away. "Let me," he said to the giant, "just make a coil of rope to bind around my head, so that the frightful weight will not cause my forehead to give way."

Atlas found this new demand reasonable, and consented to take over the burden again for a few minutes. But the deceiver was at last deceived, and Hercules picked up the apples from the ground and set out on his way back. He carried the apples to Eurystheus, who, since his object of getting rid of the hero had not been accomplished, gave them back to Hercules as a present. The latter laid them on the altar of Minerva; but the goddess, knowing that it was contrary to the divine wishes to carry away this sacred fruit, returned the apples to the garden of the Hesperides.

The Twelfth Labor

Instead of destroying his hated enemy the labors which Eurystheus had imposed upon Hercules had only strengthened the hero in the fame for which fate had selected him. He had become the protector of all the wronged upon earth, and the boldest adventurer among mortals.

But the last labor he was to undertake in the region in which his hero strength—so the impious king hoped—would not accompany him. This was a fight with the dark powers of the underworld. He was to bring forth from Hades Cerberus, the dog of Hell. This animal had three heads with frightful jaws, from which incessantly poison flowed. A dragon's tail hung from his body, and the hair of his head and of his back formed hissing, coiling serpents.

To prepare himself for this fearful journey Hercules went to the city of Eleusis, in Attic territory, where, from a wise priest, he received secret instruction in the things of the upper and lower world, and where also he received pardon for the murder of the Centaur.

Then, with strength to meet the horrors of the underworld, Hercules traveled on to Peloponnesus, and to the Laconian city of Taenarus, which contained the opening to the lower world. Here, accompanied by Mercury, he descended through a cleft in the earth, and came to the entrance of the city of King Pluto. The shades which sadly wandered back and forth before the gates of the city took flight as soon as they caught sight of flesh and blood in the form of a living man. Only the Gorgon Medusa and the spirit of Meleager remained. The former Hercules wished to overthrow with his sword, but Mercury touched him on the arm and told him that the souls of the departed were only empty shadow pictures and could not be wounded by mortal weapons.

With the soul of Meleager the hero chatted in friendly fashion, and received from him loving messages for the upper world. Still nearer to the gates of Hades Hercules caught sight of his friends Theseus and Pirithous. When both saw the friendly form of Hercules they stretched beseeching hands towards him, trembling with the hope that through his strength they might again reach the upper world. Hercules grasped Theseus by the hand, freed him from his chains and raised him from the ground. A second attempt to free Pirithous did not succeed, for the ground opened beneath his feet.

At the gate of the City of the Dead stood King Pluto, and denied entrance to Hercules. But with an arrow the hero shot the god in the shoulder, so that he feared the mortal; and when Hercules then asked whether he might lead away the dog of Hades he did not longer oppose him. But he imposed the condition that Hercules should become master of Cerberus without using any weapons. So the hero set out, protected only with cuirass and the lion skin.

He found the dog camping near the dwelling of Acheron, and without paying any attention to the bellowing of the three heads, which was like the echo of fearful resounding thunder, he seized the dog by the legs, put his arms around his neck, and would not let him go, although the dragon tail of the animal bit him in the cheek.

He held the neck of Cerberus firm, and did not let go until he was really master of the monster. Then he raised it, and through another opening of Hades returned in happiness to his own country. When the dog of Hades saw the light of day he was afraid and began to spit poison, from which poisonous plants sprung up out of the earth. Hercules brought the monster in chains to Tirynth, and led it before the astonished Eurystheus, who could not believe his eyes.

Now at last the king doubted whether he could ever rid himself of the hated son of Jupiter. He yielded to his fate and dismissed the hero, who led the dog of Hades back to his owner in the lower world.

Thus Hercules after all his labors was at last set free from the service of Eurystheus, and returned to Thebes.

Deucalion And Pyrrha

While the men of the Age of Bronze still dwelt upon the earth reports of their wickedness were carried to Jupiter. The god decided to verify the reports by coming to earth himself in the form of a man, and everywhere he went he found that the reports were much milder than the truth.

One evening in the late twilight he entered the inhospitable shelter of the Arcadian King Lycaon, who was famed for his wild conduct. By several signs he let it be known that he was a god, and the crowd dropped to their knees; but Lycaon made light of the pious prayers.

"Let us see," he said, "whether he is a mortal or a god."

Thereupon he decided to destroy the guest that night while he lay in slumber, not expecting death. But before doing so he killed a poor hostage whom the Molossians had sent to him, cooked the half-living limbs in boiling water or broiled them over a fire, and placed them on the table before the guest for his evening meal.

But Jupiter, who knew all this, left the table and sent a raging fire over the castle of the godless man. Frightened, the king fled into the open field. The first cry he uttered was a howl;

his garments changed to fur; his arms to legs; he was transformed into a bloodthirsty wolf.

Jupiter returned to Olympus, held counsel with the gods and decided to destroy the reckless race of men. At first he wanted to turn his lightnings over all the earth, but the fear that the ether would take fire and destroy the axle of the universe restrained him. He laid aside the thunderbolt which the Cyclops had fashioned for him, and decided to send rain from heaven over all the earth and so destroy the race of mortals.

Immediately the North Wind and all the other cloud-scattering winds were locked in the cave of Aeolus, and only the South Wind sent out. The latter descended upon the earth; his frightful face was covered with darkness; his beard was heavy with clouds; from his white hair ran the flood; mists lay upon his brow; from his bosom dropped the water. The South Wind grasped the heavens, seized in his hands the surrounding clouds and began to squeeze them. The thunder rolled; floods of rain burst from the heavens. The standing corn was bent to the earth; destroyed was the hope of the farmer; destroyed the weary work of a whole year.

Even Neptune, god of the sea, came to the assistance of his brother Jupiter in the work of destruction. He called all the rivers together and said, "Give full rein to your torrents; enter houses; break through all dams!"

They followed his command, and Neptune himself struck the earth with his trident and let the flood enter. Then the waters streamed over the open meadows, covered the fields, dislodged trees, temples and houses. Wherever a palace stood, its gables were soon covered with water and the highest turrets were hidden in the torrent. Sea and earth were no longer divided; all was flood—an unbroken stretch of water.

Men tried to save themselves as best they could; some climbed the high mountains; others entered boats and rowed, now over the roofs of the fallen houses, now over the hills of their ruined vineyards. Fish swam among the branches of the highest trees; the wild boar was caught in the flood; people were swept away by the water and those whom the flood spared died of hunger on the barren mountains.

One high mountain in the country of Phocis still raised two peaks above the surrounding waters. It was the great Mount Parnassus. Toward this floated a boat containing Deucalion, the son of Prometheus, and his wife Pyrrha. No man, no woman, had ever been found who surpassed these in righteousness and piety. When, therefore, Jupiter, looking down from heaven upon the earth, saw that only a single pair of mortals remained of the many thousand times a thousand, both blameless, both devoted servants of the gods, he sent forth the North Wind, recalled the clouds, and once again separated the earth from the heavens and the heavens from the earth.

Even Neptune, lord of the sea, laid down his trident and calmed the flood. The ocean resumed its banks; the rivers returned to their beds; forests stretched their slime-covered tree-tops out of the deep; hills followed; finally stretches of level land appeared and the earth was as before.

Deucalion looked around him. The country was laid waste; it was wrapped in the silence of the grave. Tears rolled down his cheeks and he said to his wife, Pyrrha, "Beloved, solitary companion of my life, as far as I can see through all the surrounding country, I can discover no living creature. We two must people the earth; all the rest have been drowned by the flood. But even we are not yet certain of our lives. Every cloud that I see strikes terror to my soul. And even if danger is past, what shall we do alone on the forsaken earth? Oh, that my father Prometheus had taught me the art of creating men and breathing life into them!"

Then the two began to weep. They threw themselves on their knees before the half-destroyed altar of the goddess Themis, and began to pray, saying, "Tell us, O goddess, by what means we can replace the race that has disappeared? Oh, help the earth to new life."

"Leave my altar," sounded the voice of the goddess. "Uncover your heads, ungird your garments and cast the bones of your mother behind you."

For a long time Deucalion and Pyrrha wondered over the puzzling words of the goddess. Pyrrha was the first to break the silence. "Pardon me, O noble goddess," she said, "if I do not obey you and cannot consent to scatter the bones of my mother."

Then Deucalion had a happy thought. He comforted his wife. "Either my reason deceives me," he said, "or the command of the goddess is good and involves no impiety. The great mother of all of us is the Earth; her bones are the stones, and these, Pyrrha, we will cast behind us!"

Both mistrusted this interpretation of the words, but what harm would it do to try? Thereupon they uncovered their heads, ungirded their garments and began casting stones behind them.

Then a wonderful thing happened. The stone began to lose its hardness, became malleable, grew and took form—not definite at once, but rude figures such as an artist first hews out of the rough marble. Whatever was moist or earthy in the stones was changed into flesh; the harder parts became bones; the veins in the rock remained as veins in the bodies. Thus, in a little while, with the aid of the gods, the stones which Deucalion threw assumed the form of men; those which Pyrrha threw, the form of women.

This homely origin the race of men does not deny; they are a hardy people, accustomed to work. Every moment of the day they remember from what sturdy stock they have sprung.

new humans created

Theseus And The Centaur

Theseus, the hero king of Athens, had a reputation for great strength and bravery; but Pirithous, the son of Ixion, one of the most famous heroes of antiquity, wished to put him to the test. He therefore drove the cattle which belonged to Theseus away from Marathon, and when he heard that Theseus, weapon in hand, was following him, then, indeed, he had what he desired. He did not flee, but turned around to meet him.

When the two heroes were near enough to see each other, each was so filled with admiration for the beautiful form and the bravery of his opponent that, as if at a given signal, both threw down their weapons and hastened toward each other. Pirithous extended his hand to Theseus and proposed that the latter act as arbitrator for the settlement of the dispute about the cattle: whatever satisfaction Theseus would demand Pirithous would willingly give.

"The only satisfaction which I desire," answered Pirithous, "is that you instead of my enemy become my friend and comrade in arms."

Then the two heroes embraced each other and swore eternal friendship.

Soon after this Pirithous chose the Thessalian princess, Hippodamia, from the race of Lapithæ, for his bride, and invited Theseus to the wedding. The Lapithæ, among whom the ceremony took place, were a famous family of Thessalians, rugged mountaineers, in some respects resembling animals — the first mortals who had learned to manage a horse. But the bride, who had sprung from this race, was not at all like the men of her people. She was of noble form, with delicate youthful face, so beautiful that all the guests praised Pirithous for his good fortune.

The assembled princes of Thessaly were at the wedding feast, and also the Centaurs, relatives of Pirithous. The Centaurs were half men, the offspring which a cloud, assuming the form of the goddess Hera, had born to Ixion, the father of Pirithous. They were the eternal enemies of the Lapithæ. Upon this occasion, however, and for the sake of the bride, they had forgotten past grudges and come together to the joyful celebration. The noble castle of Pirithous resounded with glad tumult; bridal songs were sung; wine and food abounded. Indeed, there were so many guests that the palace would not accommodate all. The Lapithæ and Centaurs sat at a special table in a grotto shaded by trees.

For a long time the festivities went on with undisturbed happiness. Then the wine began to stir the heart of the wildest of the Centaurs, Eurytion, and the beauty of the Princess Hippodamia awoke in him the mad desire of robbing the bridegroom of his bride. Nobody knew how it came to pass; nobody noticed the beginning of the unthinkable act; but suddenly the guests saw the wild Eurytion lifting Hippodamia from her feet, while she struggled and cried for help. His deed was the signal for the rest of the drunken Centaurs to do likewise, and before the strange heroes and the Lapithæ could leave their places, every one of the Centaurs had roughly seized one of the Thessalian princesses who served at the court of the king or who had assembled as guests at the wedding.

The castle and the grotto resembled a besieged city; the cry of the women sounded far and wide. Quickly friends and relatives sprang from their places.

"What delusion is this, Eurytion," cried Theseus, "to vex Pirithous while I still live, and by so doing arouse the anger of two heroes?" With these words he forced his way through the crowd and tore the stolen bride from the struggling robber.

Eurytion said nothing, for he could not excuse his deed, but he lifted his hand toward Theseus and gave him a rough knock in the chest. Then Theseus, who had no weapon at hand, seized an iron jug of embossed workmanship which stood near by and flung it into the face of his opponent with such force that the Centaur fell backward on the ground, while brains and blood oozed from the wound in his head.

"To arms!" the cry arose from all sides. At first beakers, flasks and bowls flew back and forth. Then one sacrilegious monster grabbed the oblations from the neighboring apartments. Another tore down the lamp which burned over the table, while still another fought with a sacrificial deer which had hung on one side of the grotto. A frightful slaughter ensued. Rhoetus, the most wicked of the Centaurs after Eurytion, seized the largest brand from the altar and thrust it into the gaping wound of one of the fallen Lapithæ, so that the blood hissed like iron in a furnace. In opposition to him rose Dryas, the bravest of the Lapithæ, and seizing a glowing log from the fire, thrust it into the Centaur's neck. The fate of this Centaur atoned for the death of his fallen companion, and Dryas turned to the raging mob and laid five of them low.

Then the spear of the brave hero Pirithous flew forth and pierced a mighty Centaur, Petraeus, just as he was about to uproot a tree to use it for a club. The spear pinned him against the knotted oak. A second, Dictys, fell at the stroke of the Greek hero, and in falling snapped off a mighty ash tree; a third, wishing to avenge him, was crushed by Theseus with an oak club.

The most beautiful and youthful of the Centaurs was Cyllarus. His long hair and beard were golden; his smile was friendly; his neck, shoulders, hands and breast were as beautiful as if formed by an artist. Even the lower part of his body, the part which resembled a horse, was faultless, pitch-black in color, with legs and tail of lighter dye. He had come to the feast with his wife, the beautiful Centaur, Hylonome, who at the table had leaned gracefully against him and even now united with him in the raging fight. He received from an unknown hand a light wound near his heart, and sank dying in the arms of his wife. Hylonome nursed his dying form, kissed him and tried to retain the fleeting breath. When she saw that he was gone she drew a dagger from her breast and stabbed herself.

For a long time still the fight between the Lapithæ and the Centaurs continued, but at last night put an end to the tumult. Then Pirithous remained in undisturbed possession of his bride, and on the following morning Theseus departed, bidding farewell to his friend. The common fight had quickly welded the fresh tie of their brotherhood into an indestructible bond.

Niobe

Niobe, Queen of Thebes, was proud of many things. Amphion, her husband, had received from the Muses a wonderful lyre, to the music of which the stones of the royal palace had of themselves assumed place. Her father was Tantalus, who had been entertained by the gods; and she herself was the ruler of a powerful kingdom and a woman of great pride of spirit and majestic beauty. But of none of these things was she so proud as she was of her fourteen lovely children, the seven sons and seven daughters to whom she had given birth.

Indeed, Niobe was the happiest of all mothers, and so would she have remained if she had not believed herself so peculiarly blessed. Her very knowledge of her good fortune was her undoing.

One day the prophetess Manto, daughter of the soothsayer Tiresias, being instructed of the gods, called together the women of Thebes to do honor to the goddess Latona and her two children, Apollo and Diana. "Put laurel wreaths upon your heads," were her commands, "and bring sacrifices with pious prayers."

Then while the women of Thebes were gathering together, Niobe came forth, clad in a gold-embroidered garment, with a crowd of followers, radiant in her beauty, though angry, with her hair flowing about her shoulders. She stopped in the midst of the busy women, and raising her voice, spoke to them.

"Are you not foolish to worship gods of whom stories are told to you when more favored beings dwell here among you? While you are making sacrifices on the altar of Latona, why does my divine name remain unknown? My father Tantalus is the only mortal who has ever sat at the table of the gods; and my mother Dione is the sister of the Pleiades, who as bright stars shine nightly in the heavens. One of my uncles is the giant Atlas, who on his neck supports the vaulted heavens; my grandfather is Jupiter, the father of the gods. The people of Phrygia obey me, and to me and my husband belongs the city of Cadmus, the walls of which were put together by the music that my husband played. Every corner of my palace is filled with priceless treasures; and there, too, are other treasures—children such as no other mother can show: seven beautiful daughters, seven sturdy sons, and just as many sons- and daughters-in-law. Ask now whether I have ground for pride. Consider again before you honor more than me Latona, the unknown daughter of the Titans, who could find no place in the whole earth in which she might rest and give birth to her children until the island of Delos in compassion offered her a precarious shelter. There she became the mother of two children—the poor creature! Just the seventh part of my mother joy! Who can deny that I am fortunate? Who will doubt that I shall remain happy? Fortune would have a hard time if she undertook to shatter my happiness. Take this or that one from my treasured children; but when would the number of them dwindle to the sickly two of Latona? Away with your sacrifices! Take the laurel out of your hair. Go back to your homes and let me never see such foolishness again!"

Frightened at the outburst, the women removed the wreaths from their heads, left their sacrifices and slunk home, still honoring Latona with silent prayer.

On the summit of the Delian mountain Cynthas stood Latona with her two children, watching what was taking place in distant Thebes. "See, my children," she said, "I, your mother, who am so proud of your birth, who yield place to no goddess except Juno, I am held up to ridicule by an upstart mortal, and if you do not defend me, my children, I shall be driven away from the ancient and holy altars. Yes, you too are insulted by Niobe, and she would like to have you set aside for her children!"

Latona was about to go on, but Apollo interrupted her: "Cease your lamentations, mother; you only delay the punishment."

Then he and his sister wrapped themselves in a magic cloud cloak that made them invisible, and flew swiftly through the air until they reached the town and castle of Cadmus.

Just outside the walls of the city was an open field that was used as a race-course and practice ground for horses. Here the seven sons of Amphion were amusing themselves, · when suddenly the oldest dropped his reins with a cry and fell from his horse, pierced to the heart by an arrow. One after another the whole seven were struck down.

The news of the disaster soon spread through the city. Amphion, when he heard that all his sons had perished, fell on his own sword. Then the loud cries of his servants penetrated to the women's quarters.

For a long time Niobe could not believe that the gods had thus brought vengeance. When she did, how unlike was she to the Niobe who drove the people from the altars of the mighty goddess and strode through the city with haughty mien. Crazed with grief she rushed out to the field where her sons had been stricken, threw herself on their dead bodies, kissing now this one and now that. Then, raising her arms to heaven, she cried, "Look now upon my distress, thou cruel Latona; for the death of these seven bows me to the earth. Triumph thou, O my victorious enemy!"

Now the seven daughters of Niobe, clad in garments of mourning, drew near, and with loosened hair stood around their brothers. And the sight of them brought a ray of joy to Niobe's white face. She forgot her grief for a moment, and casting a scornful look to heaven, said, "Victor! No, for even in my loss I have more than thou in thy happiness!"

Hardly had she spoken when there was the sound of a drawn bow. The bystanders grew cold with fear, but Niobe was not frightened, for misfortune had made her strong.

Suddenly one of the sisters put her hand to her breast and drew out an arrow that had pierced her; then, unconscious, she sank to the ground. Another daughter hastened to her mother to comfort her, but before she could reach her she was laid low by a hidden wound. One after another the rest fell, until only the last was left. She had fled to Niobe's lap and childlike was hiding her face in her mother's garments.

"Leave me only this one," cried Niobe, "just the youngest of so many."

But even while she prayed the child fell lifeless from her lap, and Niobe sat alone among the dead bodies of her husband, her sons and her daughters. She was speechless with grief; no breath of air stirred the hair on her head; the blood left her face; the eyes remained fixed on the grief-stricken countenance; in the whole body there was no longer any sign of life. The veins ceased to carry blood; the neck stiffened; arms and feet grew rigid; the whole body was transformed into cold and lifeless stone. Nothing living remained to her except her tears, which continued flowing from her stony eyes.

Then a mighty wind lifted the image of stone, carried it over the sea and set it down in Lydia, the old home of Niobe, in the barren mountains under the stony cliffs of Sipylus. Here Niobe remained fixed as a marble statue on the summit of the mountain, and to this very day you can see the grief-stricken mother in tears.

The Gorgon's Head

Perseus was the son of Danaë, who was the daughter of a king. And when Perseus was a very little boy, some wicked people put his mother and himself into a chest and set them afloat upon the sea. The wind blew freshly and drove the chest away from the shore, and the uneasy billows tossed it up and down; while Danaë clasped her child closely to her bosom, and dreaded that some big wave would dash its foamy crest over them both. The chest sailed on, however, and neither sank nor was upset, until, when night was coming, it floated so near an island that it got entangled in a fisherman's nets and was drawn out high and dry upon the sand. This island was called Seriphus and it was reigned over by King Polydectes, who happened to be the fisherman's brother.

This fisherman, I am glad to tell you, was an exceedingly humane and upright man. He showed great kindness to Danaë and her little boy, and continued to befriend them until Perseus had grown to be a handsome youth, very strong and active and skilful in the use of arms. Long before this time King Polydectes had seen the two strangers—the mother and her child—who had come to his dominions in a floating chest. As he was not good and kind, like his brother the fisherman, but extremely wicked, he resolved to send Perseus on a dangerous enterprise, in which he would probably be killed, and then to do some great mischief to Danaë herself. So this bad-hearted king spent a long while in considering what was the most dangerous thing that a young man could possibly undertake to perform. At last, having hit upon an enterprise that promised to turn out as fatally as he desired, he sent for the youthful Perseus.

The young man came to the palace and found the king sitting upon his throne.

"Perseus," said King Polydectes, smiling craftily upon him, "you are grown up a fine young man. You and your good mother have received a great deal of kindness from myself, as well as from my worthy brother the fisherman, and I suppose you would not be sorry to repay some of it."

"Please, your Majesty," answered Perseus, "I would willingly risk my life to do so."

"Well, then," continued the king, still with a cunning smile on his lips, "I have a little adventure to propose to you, and as you are a brave and enterprising youth, you will doubtless look upon it as a great piece of good luck to have so rare an opportunity of distinguishing yourself. You must know, my good Perseus, I think of getting married to the beautiful Princess Hippodamia, and it is customary on these occasions to make the bride a present of some far-fetched and elegant curiosity. I have been a little perplexed, I must honestly confess, where to obtain anything likely to please a princess of her exquisite taste. But this morning, I flatter myself, I have thought of precisely the article."

"And can I assist your Majesty in obtaining it?" cried Perseus, eagerly.

"You can if you are as brave a youth as I believe you to be," replied King Polydectes with the utmost graciousness of manner. "The bridal gift which I have set my heart on presenting to the beautiful Hippodamia is the head of the Gorgon Medusa with the snaky locks; and I depend on you, my dear Perseus, to bring it to me. So, as I am anxious to settle affairs with the princess, the sooner you go in quest of the Gorgon, the better I shall be pleased."

"I will set out tomorrow morning," answered Perseus.

"Pray do so, my gallant youth," rejoined the king. "And, Perseus, in cutting off the Gorgon's head, be careful to make a clean stroke, so as not to injure its appearance. You must bring it home in the very best condition in order to suit the exquisite taste of the beautiful Princess Hippodamia."

Perseus left the palace, but was scarcely out of hearing before Polydectes burst into a laugh, being greatly amused, wicked king that he was, to find how readily the young man fell into the snare. The news quickly spread abroad that Perseus had undertaken to cut off the head of Medusa with the snaky locks. Everybody was rejoiced, for most of the inhabitants of the island were as wicked as the king himself and would have liked nothing better than to see some enormous mischief happen to Danaë and her son. The only good man in this unfortunate island of Seriphus appears to have been the fisherman. As Perseus walked along, therefore, the people pointed after him and made mouths, and winked to one another and ridiculed him as loudly as they dared.

"Ho, ho!" cried they; "Medusa's snakes will sting him soundly!"

Now, there were three Gorgons alive at that period, and they were the most strange and terrible monsters that had ever been since the world was made, or that have been seen in after days, or that are likely to be seen in all time to come. I hardly know what sort of creature or hobgoblin to call them. They were three sisters and seem to have borne some distant resemblance to women, but were really a very frightful and mischievous species of dragon. It is, indeed, difficult to imagine what hideous beings these three sisters were. Why, instead of locks of hair, if you can believe men, they had each of them a hundred enormous snakes growing on their heads, all alive, twisting, wriggling, curling and thrusting out their venomous tongues, with forked stings at the end! The teeth of the Gorgons were terribly long tusks, their hands were made of brass, and their bodies were all over scales, which, if not iron, were something as hard and impenetrable. They had wings, too, and exceedingly splendid ones, I can assure you, for every feather in them was pure, bright, glittering, burnished gold; and they looked very dazzling, no doubt, when the Gorgons were flying about in the sunshine.

But when people happened to catch a glimpse of their glittering brightness, aloft in the air, they seldom stopped to gaze, but ran and hid themselves as speedily as they could. You will think, perhaps, that they were afraid of being stung by the serpents that served the Gorgons instead of hair—or of having their heads bitten off by their ugly tusks—or of being torn all to pieces by their brazen claws. Well, to be sure, these were some of the dangers, but by no means the greatest nor the most difficult to avoid. For the worst thing about these abominable Gorgons was that if once a poor mortal fixed his eyes full upon one of their faces, he was certain that very instant to be changed from warm flesh and blood into cold and lifeless stone!

Thus, as you will easily perceive, it was a very dangerous adventure that the wicked King Polydectes had contrived for this innocent young man. Perseus himself, when he had thought over the matter, could not help seeing that he had very little chance of coming safely through it, and that he was far more likely to become a stone image than to bring back the head of Medusa with the snaky locks. For, not to speak of other difficulties, there was one which it would have puzzled an older man than Perseus to get over. Not only must he fight with and slay this golden-winged, iron-scaled, long-tusked, brazen-clawed, snaky-haired monster, but he must do it with his eyes shut, or, at least, without so much as a glance at the enemy with whom he was contending. Else, while his arm was lifted to strike, he would stiffen into stone and stand with that uplifted arm for centuries, until time and the wind and weather should crumble him quite away. This would be a very sad thing to befall a young man who wanted to perform a great many brave deeds and to enjoy a great deal of happiness in this bright and beautiful world.

So disconsolate did these thoughts make him that Perseus could not bear to tell his mother what he had undertaken to do.

He therefore took his shield, girded on his sword and crossed over from the island to the mainland, where he sat down in a solitary place and hardly refrained from shedding tears.

But while he was in this sorrowful mood, he heard a voice close beside him.

"Perseus," said the voice, "why are you sad?"

He lifted his head from his hands, in which he had hidden it, and behold! all alone as Perseus had supposed himself to be, there was a stranger in the solitary place. It was a brisk, intelligent and remarkably shrewd-looking young man, with a cloak over his shoulders, an odd sort of cap on his head, a strangely twisted staff in his hand and a short and very crooked sword hanging by his side. He was exceedingly light and active in his figure, like a person much accustomed to gymnastic exercises and well able to leap or run. Above all, the stranger had such a cheerful, knowing and helpful aspect (though it was certainly a little mischievous, into the bargain) that Perseus could not help feeling his spirits grow livelier as he gazed at him. Besides, being really a courageous youth, he felt greatly ashamed that anybody should have found him with tears in his eyes like a timid little schoolboy, when, after all, there might be no occasion for despair. So Perseus wiped his eyes and answered the stranger pretty briskly, putting on as brave a look as he could.

"I am not so very sad," said he, "only thoughtful about an adventure that I have undertaken."

"Oho!" answered the stranger. "Well, tell me all about it and possibly I may be of service to you. I have helped a good many young men through adventures that looked difficult enough beforehand. Perhaps you may have heard of me. I have more names than one, but the name of Quicksilver suits me as well as any other. Tell me what the trouble is and we will talk the matter over and see what can be done."

The stranger's words and manner put Perseus into quite a different mood from his former one. He resolved to tell Quicksilver all his difficulties, since he could not easily be worse off than he already was, and, very possibly, his new friend might give him some advice that would turn out well in the end. So he let the stranger know in few words precisely what was the case—how the King Polydectes wanted the head of Medusa with the snaky locks as a bridal gift for the beautiful Princess Hippodamia and how that he had undertaken to get it for him, but was afraid of being turned into stone.

"And that would be a great pity," said Quicksilver, with his mischievous smile. "You would make a very handsome marble statue, it is true, and it would be a considerable number of centuries before you crumbled away; but, on the whole, one would rather be a young man for a few years than a stone image for a great many."

"Oh, far rather!" exclaimed Perseus, with the tears again standing in his eyes. "And, besides, what would my dear mother do if her beloved son were turned into a stone?"

"Well, well, let us hope that the affair will not turn out so very badly," replied Quicksilver in an encouraging tone. "I am the very person to help you, if anybody can. My sister and myself will do our utmost to bring you safe through the adventure, ugly as it now looks."

"Your sister?" repeated Perseus.

"Yes, my sister," said the stranger. "She is very wise, I promise you; and as for myself, I generally have all my wits about me, such as they are. If you show yourself bold and cautious, and follow our advice, you need not fear being a stone image yet awhile. But, first of all, you must polish your shield till you can see your face in it as distinctly as in a mirror."

This seemed to Perseus rather an odd beginning of the adventure, for he thought it of far more consequence that the shield should be strong enough to defend him from the Gorgon's brazen claws than that it should be bright enough to show him the reflection of his face. However, concluding that Quicksilver knew better than himself, he immediately set to work and scrubbed the shield with so much diligence and good will that it very quickly shone like the moon at harvest time. Quicksilver looked at it with a smile and nodded his approbation. Then taking off his own short and crooked sword, he girded it about Perseus, instead of the one which he had before worn.

"No sword but mine will answer your purpose," observed he; "the blade has a most excellent temper and will cut through iron and brass as easily as through the slenderest twig. And now we will set out. The next thing is to find the Three Gray Women, who will tell us where to find the Nymphs."

"The Three Gray Women!" cried Perseus, to whom this seemed only a new difficulty in the path of his adventure. "Pray, who may the Three Gray Women be? I never heard of them before."

"They are three very strange old ladies," said Quicksilver, laughing. "They have but one eye among them, and only one tooth. Moreover, you must find them out by starlight or in the dusk of the evening, for they never show themselves by the light either of the sun or moon."

"But," said Perseus, "why should I waste my time with these Three Gray Women? Would it not be better to set out at once in search of the terrible Gorgons?"

"No, no," answered his friend. "There are other things to be done before you can find your way to the Gorgons. There is nothing for it but to hunt up these old ladies; and when we meet with them, you may be sure that the Gorgons are not a great way off. Come, let us be stirring!"

Perseus by this time felt so much confidence in his companion's sagacity that he made no more objections, and professed himself ready to begin the adventure immediately. They accordingly set out and walked at a pretty brisk pace; so brisk, indeed, that Perseus found it rather difficult to keep up with his nimble friend Quicksilver. To say the truth, he had a singular idea that Quicksilver was furnished with a pair of winged shoes, which, of course, helped him along marvelously. And then, too, when Perseus looked sideways at him out of the corner of his eye, he seemed to see wings on the side of his head; although, if he turned a full gaze, there were no such things to be perceived, but only an odd kind of cap. But at all events, the twisted staff was evidently a great convenience to

Quicksilver, and enabled him to proceed so fast that Perseus, though a remarkably active young man, began to be out of breath.

"Here!" cried Quicksilver at last—for he knew well enough, rogue that he was, how hard Perseus found it to keep pace with him—"take you the staff, for you need it a great deal more than I. Are there no better walkers than yourself in the island of Seriphus?"

"I could walk pretty well," said Perseus, glancing slyly at his companion's feet, "if I had only a pair of winged shoes."

"We must see about getting you a pair," answered Quicksilver.

But the staff helped Perseus along so bravely that he no longer felt the slightest weariness. In fact, the stick seemed to be alive in his hand and to lend some of its life to Perseus. He and Quicksilver now walked onward at their ease, talking very sociably together; and Quicksilver told so many pleasant stories about his former adventures and how well his wits had served him on various occasions that Perseus began to think him a very wonderful person. He evidently knew the world; and nobody is so charming to a young man as a friend who has that kind of knowledge. Perseus listened the more eagerly, in the hope of brightening his own wits by what he heard.

At last, he happened to recollect that Quicksilver had spoken of a sister who was to lend her assistance in the adventure which they were now bound upon.

"Where is she?" he inquired. "Shall we not meet her soon?"

"All at the proper time," said his companion. "But this sister of mine, you must understand, is quite a different sort of character from myself. She is very grave and prudent, seldom smiles, never laughs and makes it a rule not to utter a word unless she has something particularly profound to say. Neither will she listen to any but the wisest conversation."

"Dear me!" ejaculated Perseus; "I shall be afraid to say a syllable."

"She is a very accomplished person, I assure you," continued Quicksilver, "and has all the arts and science at her fingers' ends. In short, she is so immoderately wise that many people call her wisdom personified. But to tell you the truth, she has hardly vivacity enough for my taste; and I think you would scarcely find her so pleasant a traveling companion as myself. She has her good points, nevertheless; and you will find the benefit of them in your encounter with the Gorgons."

By this time it had grown quite dusk. They were now come to a very wild and desert place, overgrown with shaggy bushes and so silent and solitary that nobody seemed ever to have dwelt or journeyed there. All was waste and desolate in the gray twilight, which grew every moment more obscure. Perseus looked about him rather disconsolately and asked Quicksilver whether they had a great deal farther to go.

"Hist! hist!" whispered his companion. "Make no noise! This is just the time and place to meet the Three Gray Women. Be careful that they do not see you before you see them, for though they have but a single eye among the three, it is as sharp-sighted as half a dozen common eyes."

"But what must I do," asked Perseus, "when we meet them?"

Quicksilver explained to Perseus how the Three Gray Women managed with their one eye. They were in the habit, it seems, of changing it from one to another, as if it had been a pair of spectacles, or — which would have suited them better — a quizzing glass. When one of the three had kept the eye a certain time, she took it out of the socket and passed it to one of her sisters, whose turn it might happen to be, and who immediately clapped it into her own head and enjoyed a peep at the visible world. Thus it will easily be understood that only one of the Three Gray Women could see, while the other two were in utter darkness; and, moreover, at the instant when the eye was passing from hand to hand, none of the poor old ladies was able to see a wink. I have heard of a great many strange things in my day, and have witnessed not a few, but none, it seems to me, that can compare with the oddity of these Three Gray Women all peeping through a single eye.

So thought Perseus, likewise, and was so astonished that he almost fancied his companion was joking with him, and that there were no such old women in the world.

"You will soon find whether I tell the truth or no," observed Quicksilver. "Hark! hush! hist! hist! There they come now!"

Perseus looked earnestly through the dusk of the evening, and there, sure enough, at no great distance off, he descried the Three Gray Women. The light being so faint, he could not well make out what sort of figures they were; only he discovered that they had long gray hair, and as they came nearer he saw that two of them had but the empty socket of an eye in the middle of their foreheads. But in the middle of the third sister's forehead there was a very large, bright and piercing eye, which sparkled like a great diamond in a ring; and so penetrating did it seem to be that Perseus could not help thinking it must possess the gift of seeing in the darkest midnight just as perfectly as at noonday. The sight of three persons' eyes was melted and collected into that single one.

Thus the three old dames got along about as comfortably, upon the whole, as if they could all see at once. She who chanced to have the eye in her forehead led the other two by the hands, peeping sharply about her all the while; insomuch that Perseus dreaded lest she should see right through the thick clump of bushes behind which he and Quicksilver had hidden themselves. My stars! It was positively terrible to be within reach of so very sharp an eye!

But before they reached the clump of bushes, one of the Three Gray Women spoke.

"Sister! Sister Scarecrow!" cried she, "you have had the eye long enough. It is my turn now!"

"Let me keep it a moment longer, Sister Nightmare," answered Scarecrow. "I thought I had a glimpse of something behind that thick bush."

"Well, and what of that?" retorted Nightmare, peevishly. "Can't I see into a thick bush as easily as yourself? The eye is mine as well as yours; and I know the use of it as well as you, or maybe a little better. I insist upon taking a peep immediately!"

But here the third sister, whose name was Shakejoint, began to complain, and said that it was her turn to have the eye, and that Scarecrow and Nightmare wanted to keep it all to themselves. To end the dispute, old Dame Scarecrow took the eye out of her forehead and held it forth in her hand.

"Take it, one of you," cried she, "and quit this foolish quarreling. For my part, I shall be glad of a little thick darkness. Take it quickly, however, or I must clap it into my own head again!"

Accordingly, both Nightmare and Shakejoint put out their hands, groping eagerly to snatch the eye out of the hand of Scarecrow. But being both alike blind, they could not easily find where Scarecrow's hand was; and Scarecrow, being now just as much in the dark as Shakejoint and Nightmare, could not at once meet either of their hands in order to put the eye into it. Thus (as you will see with half an eye, my wise little auditors) these good old dames had fallen into a strange perplexity. For, though the eye shone and glistened like a star as Scarecrow held it out, yet the Gray Women caught not the least glimpse of its light and were all three in utter darkness from too impatient a desire to see.

Quicksilver was so much tickled at beholding Shakejoint and Nightmare both groping for the eye, and each finding fault with Scarecrow and one another, that he could scarcely help laughing aloud.

"Now is your time!" he whispered to Perseus. "Quick, quick! before they can clap the eye into either of their heads. Rush out upon the old ladies and snatch it from Scarecrow's hand!"

In an instant, while the Three Gray Women were still scolding each other, Perseus leaped from behind the clump of bushes and made himself master of the prize. The marvelous eye, as he held it in his hand, shone very brightly, and seemed to look up into his face with a knowing air, and an expression as if it would have winked had it been provided with a pair of eyelids for that purpose. But the Gray Women knew nothing of what had happened, and each supposing that one of her sisters was in possession of the eye, they began their quarrel anew. At last, as Perseus did not wish to put these respectable dames to greater inconvenience than was really necessary, he thought it right to explain the matter.

"My good ladies," said he, "pray do not be angry with one another. If anybody is in fault, it is myself; for I have the honor to hold your very brilliant and excellent eye in my own hand!"

"You! You have our eye! And who are you?" screamed the Three Gray Women all in a breath; for they were terribly frightened, of course, at hearing a strange voice and discovering that their eyesight had got into the hands of they could not guess whom. "Oh, what shall we do, sisters? what shall we do? We are all in the dark! Give us our eye! Give us our one precious, solitary eye! You have two of your own! Give us our eye!"

"Tell them," whispered Quicksilver to Perseus, "that they shall have back the eye as soon as they direct you where to find the Nymphs who have the flying slippers, the magic wallet and the helmet of darkness."

"My dear, good, admirable old ladies," said Perseus, addressing the Gray Women, "there is no occasion for putting yourselves into such a fright. I am by no means a bad young man. You shall have back your eye, safe and sound, and as bright as ever, the moment you tell me where to find the Nymphs."

"The Nymphs! Goodness me! Sisters, what Nymphs does he mean?" screamed Scarecrow. "There are a great many Nymphs, people say; some that go a hunting in the woods, and some that live inside of trees, and some that have a comfortable home in fountains of water. We know nothing at all about them. We are three unfortunate old souls that go wandering about in the dusk and never had but one eye amongst us, and that one you have stolen away. Oh, give it back, good stranger! — whoever you are, give it back!"

All this while the Three Gray Women were groping with their outstretched hands and trying their utmost to get hold of Perseus. But he took good care to keep out of their reach.

"My respectable dames," said he—for his mother had taught him always to use the greatest civility—"I hold your eye fast in my hand and shall keep it safely for you until you please to tell me where to find these Nymphs. The Nymphs, I mean, who keep the enchanted wallet, the flying slippers and the what is it?—the helmet of invisibility."

"Mercy on us, sisters! what is the young man talking about?" exclaimed Scarecrow, Nightmare and Shakejoint, one to another, with great appearance of astonishment. "A pair of flying slippers, quoth he! His heels would quickly fly higher than his head if he was silly enough to put them on. And a helmet of invisibility! How could a helmet make him invisible, unless it were big enough for him to hide under it? And an enchanted wallet! What sort of a contrivance may that be, I wonder? No, no, good stranger! we can tell you nothing of these marvelous things. You have two eyes of your own and we have but a single one amongst us three. You can find out such wonders better than three blind old creatures like us."

Perseus, hearing them talk in this way, began really to think that the Gray Women knew nothing of the matter; and, as it grieved him to put them to so much trouble, he was just on the point of restoring their eye and asking pardon for his rudeness in snatching it away. But Quicksilver caught his hand.

"Don't let them make a fool of you!" said he. "These Three Gray Women are the only persons in the world that can tell you where to find the Nymphs, and unless you get that information you will never succeed in cutting off the head of Medusa with the snaky locks. Keep fast hold on the eye and all will go well."

As it turned out, Quicksilver was in the right. There are but few things that people prize so much as they do their eyesight; and the Gray Women valued their single eye as highly as if it had been half a dozen, which was the number they ought to have had. Finding that there was no other way of recovering it, they at last told Perseus what he wanted to know. No sooner had they done so than he immediately and with the utmost respect clapped the eye into the vacant socket in one of their foreheads, thanked them for their kindness and bade them farewell. Before the young man was out of hearing, however, they had got into a new dispute, because he happened to have given the eye to Scarecrow, who had already taken her turn of it when their trouble with Perseus commenced.

It is greatly to be feared that the Three Gray Women were very much in the habit of disturbing their mutual harmony by bickerings of this sort, which was the more pity, as they could not conveniently do without one another and were evidently intended to be inseparable companions. As a general rule, I would advise all people, whether sisters or brothers, old or young, who chance to have but one eye amongst them, to cultivate forbearance and not all insist upon peeping through it at once.

Quicksilver and Perseus, in the meantime, were making the best of their way in quest of the Nymphs. The old dames had given them such particular directions that they were not long in finding them out. They proved to be very different persons from Nightmare, Shakejoint and Scarecrow; for, instead of being old, they were young and beautiful; and instead of one eye amongst the sisterhood, each Nymph had two exceedingly bright eyes of her own, with which she looked very kindly at Perseus. They seemed to be acquainted with Quicksilver, and when he told them the adventure which Perseus had undertaken, they made no difficulty about giving him the valuable articles that were in their custody. In the first place, they brought out what appeared to be a small purse, made of deer skin and curiously embroidered, and bade him be sure and keep it safe. This was the magic wallet. The Nymphs next produced a pair of shoes or slippers or sandals, with a nice little pair of wings at the heel of each.

"Put them on, Perseus," said Quicksilver. "You will find yourself as light-heeled as you can desire for the remainder of our journey."

So Perseus proceeded to put one of the slippers on, while he laid the other on the ground by his side. Unexpectedly, however, this other slipper spread its wings, fluttered up off the ground and would probably have flown away if Quicksilver had not made a leap and luckily caught it in the air.

"Be more careful," said he as he gave it back to Perseus. "It would frighten the birds up aloft if they should see a flying slipper amongst them."

When Perseus had got on both of these wonderful slippers, he was altogether too buoyant to tread on earth. Making a step or two, lo and behold! upward he popped into the air high above the heads of Quicksilver and the Nymphs, and found it very difficult to clamber down again. Winged slippers and all such high-flying contrivances are seldom quite easy to manage until one grows a little accustomed to them. Quicksilver laughed at his companion's involuntary activity and told him that he must not be in so desperate a hurry, but must wait for the invisible helmet.

The good-natured Nymphs had the helmet, with its dark tuft of waving plumes, all in readiness to put upon his head. And now there happened about as wonderful an incident as anything that I have yet told you. The instant before the helmet was put on, there stood Perseus, a beautiful young man, with golden ringlets and rosy cheeks, the crooked sword by his side and the brightly polished shield upon his arm—a figure that seemed all made up of courage, sprightliness and glorious light. But when the helmet had descended over his white brow, there was no longer any Perseus to be seen! Nothing but empty air! Even the helmet that covered him with its invisibility had vanished!

"Where are you, Perseus?" asked Quicksilver.

"Why, here, to be sure!" answered Perseus very quietly, although his voice seemed to come out of the transparent atmosphere. "Just where I was a moment ago. Don't you see me?"

"No, indeed!" answered his friend. "You are hidden under the helmet. But if I cannot see you, neither can the Gorgons. Follow me, therefore, and we will try your dexterity in using the winged slippers."

With these words, Quicksilver's cap spread its wings, as if his head were about to fly away from his shoulders; but his whole figure rose lightly into the air and Perseus followed. By the time they had ascended a few hundred feet the young man began to feel what a delightful thing it was to leave the dull earth so far beneath him and to be able to flit about like a bird.

It was now deep night. Perseus looked upward and saw the round, bright, silvery moon and thought that he should desire nothing better than to soar up thither and spend his life there. Then he looked downward again and saw the earth, with its seas and lakes, and the silver course of its rivers, and its snowy mountain peaks, and the breath of its fields, and the dark cluster of its woods, and its cities of white marble; and with the moonshine sleeping over the whole scene, it was as beautiful as the moon or any star could be. And among other objects he saw the island of Seriphus, where his dear mother was. Sometimes he and Quicksilver approached a cloud that at a distance looked as if it were made of fleecy silver, although when they plunged into it they found themselves chilled and moistened with gray mist. So swift was their flight, however, that in an instant they emerged from the cloud into the moonlight again. Once a high-soaring eagle flew right against the invisible Perseus. The bravest sights were the meteors that gleamed suddenly out as if a bonfire had been kindled in the sky and made the moonshine pale for as much as a hundred miles around them.

As the two companions flew onward, Perseus fancied that he could hear the rustle of a garment close by his side; and it was on the side opposite to the one where he beheld Quicksilver, yet only Quicksilver was visible.

"Whose garment is this," inquired Perseus, "that keeps rustling close beside me in the breeze?"

"Oh, it is my sister's!" answered Quicksilver. "She is coming along with us, as I told you she would. We could do nothing without the help of my sister. You have no idea how wise she is. She has such eyes, too! Why, she can see you at this moment just as distinctly as if you were not invisible, and I'll venture to say she will be the first to discover the Gorgons."

By this time, in their swift voyage through the air, they had come within sight of the great ocean and were soon flying over it. Far beneath them the waves tossed themselves tumultuously in mid-sea, or rolled a white surf line upon the long beaches, or foamed against the rocky cliffs, with a roar that was thunderous in the lower world, although it became a gentle murmur, like the voice of a baby half asleep, before it reached the ears of Perseus. Just then a voice spoke in the air close by him. It seemed to be a woman's voice and was melodious, though not exactly what might be called sweet, but grave and mild.

"Perseus," said the voice, "there are the Gorgons."

"Where?" exclaimed Perseus. "I cannot see them."

"On the shore of that island beneath you," replied the voice. "A pebble dropped from your hand would strike in the midst of them."

"I told you she would be the first to discover them," said Quicksilver to Perseus. "And there they are!"

Straight downward, two or three thousand feet below him, Perseus perceived a small island, with the sea breaking into white foam all around its rocky shore, except on one side, where there was a beach of snowy sand. He descended toward it, and looking earnestly at a cluster or heap of brightness at the foot of a precipice of black rocks, behold, there were the terrible Gorgons! They lay fast asleep, soothed by the thunder of the sea; for it required a tumult that would have deafened everybody else to lull such fierce creatures into slumber. The moonlight glistened on their steely scales and on their golden wings, which drooped idly over the sand. Their brazen claws, horrible to look at, were thrust out and clutched the wave-beaten fragments of rock, while the sleeping Gorgons dreamed of tearing some poor mortal all to pieces. The snakes that served them instead of hair seemed likewise to be asleep, although now and then one would writhe and lift its head and thrust out its forked tongue, emitting a drowsy hiss, and then let itself subside among its sister snakes.

The Gorgons were more like an awful, gigantic kind of insect—immense, golden-winged beetles or dragonflies or things of that sort—at once ugly and beautiful—than like anything else; only that they were a thousand and a million times as big. And with all this there was something partly human about them, too. Luckily for Perseus, their faces were completely hidden from him by the posture in which they lay, for had he but looked one instant at them, he would have fallen heavily out of the air, an image of senseless stone.

"Now," whispered Quicksilver as he hovered by the side of Perseus—"now is your time to do the deed! Be quick, for if one of the Gorgons should awake, you are too late!"

"Which shall I strike at?" asked Perseus, drawing his sword and descending a little lower. "They all three look alike. All three have snaky locks. Which of the three is Medusa?"

It must be understood that Medusa was the only one of these dragon monsters whose head Perseus could possibly cut off. As for the other two, let him have the sharpest sword that ever was forged, and he might have hacked away by the hour together without doing them the least harm.

"Be cautious," said the calm voice which had before spoken to him. "One of the Gorgons is stirring in her sleep and is just about to turn over. That is Medusa. Do not look at her! The sight would turn you to stone! Look at the reflection of her face and figure in the bright mirror of your shield."

Perseus now understood Quicksilver's motive for so earnestly exhorting him to polish his shield. In its surface he could safely look at the reflection of the Gorgon's face. And there it was—that terrible countenance—mirrored in the brightness of the shield, with the moonlight falling over it and displaying all its horror. The snakes, whose venomous natures could not altogether sleep, kept twisting themselves over the forehead. It was the fiercest and most horrible face that ever was seen or imagined, and yet with a strange, fearful and savage kind of beauty in it. The eyes were closed and the Gorgon was still in a deep slumber; but there was an unquiet expression disturbing her features, as if the monster was troubled with an ugly dream. She gnashed her white tusks and dug into the sand with her brazen claws.

The snakes, too, seemed to feel Medusa's dream and to be made more restless by it. They twined themselves into tumultuous knots, writhed fiercely and uplifted a hundred hissing heads without opening their eyes.

"Now, now!" whispered Quicksilver, who was growing impatient. "Make a dash at the monster!"

"But be calm," said the grave, melodious voice at the young man's side. "Look in your shield as you fly downward, and take care that you do not miss your first stroke."

Perseus flew cautiously downward, still keeping his eyes on Medusa's face, as reflected in his shield. The nearer he came, the more terrible did the snaky visage and metallic body of the monster grow. At last, when he found himself hovering over her within arm's length, Perseus uplifted his sword, while at the same instant each separate snake upon the Gorgon's head stretched threateningly upward, and Medusa unclosed her eyes. But she awoke too late. The sword was sharp, the stroke fell like a lightning flash, and the head of the wicked Medusa tumbled from her body!

"Admirably done!" cried Quicksilver. "Make haste and clap the head into your magic wallet."

To the astonishment of Perseus, the small, embroidered wallet which he had hung about his neck and which had hitherto been no bigger than a purse, grew all at once large enough to contain Medusa's head. As quick as thought, he snatched it up, with the snakes still writhing upon it, and thrust it in.

"Your task is done," said the calm voice. "Now fly, for the other Gorgons will do their utmost to take vengeance for Medusa's death."

It was, indeed, necessary to take flight, for Perseus had not done the deed so quietly but that the clash of his sword and the hissing of the snakes and the thump of Medusa's head as it tumbled upon the sea-beaten sand awoke the other two monsters. There they sat for an instant, sleepily rubbing their eyes with their brazen fingers, while all the snakes on their heads reared themselves on end with surprise and with venomous malice against they knew not what. But when the Gorgons saw the scaly carcass of Medusa, headless, and her golden wings all ruffled and half spread out on the sand, it was really awful to hear what yells and screeches they set up. And then the snakes! They sent forth a hundredfold hiss with one consent, and Medusa's snakes answered them out of the magic wallet.

No sooner were the Gorgons broad awake than they hurtled upward into the air, brandishing their brass talons, gnashing their horrible tusks and flapping their huge wings so wildly that some of the golden feathers were shaken out and floated down upon the shore. And there, perhaps, those very feathers lie scattered till this day. Up rose the Gorgons, as I tell you, staring horribly about, in hopes of turning somebody to stone. Had Perseus looked them in the face or had he fallen into their clutches, his poor mother would never have kissed her boy again! But he took good care to turn his eyes another way; and as he wore the helmet of invisibility, the Gorgons knew not in what direction to follow him; nor did he fail to make the best use of the winged slippers by soaring upward a perpendicular mile or so. At that height, when the screams of those abominable creatures sounded faintly beneath him, he made a straight course for the island of Seriphus, in order to carry Medusa's head to King Polydectes.

I have no time to tell you of several marvelous things that befell Perseus on his way homeward, such as his killing a hideous sea monster just as it was on the point of devouring a beautiful maiden, nor how he changed an enormous giant into a mountain of stone merely by showing him the head of the Gorgon. If you doubt this latter story, you may make a voyage to Africa some day or other and see the very mountain, which is still known by the ancient giant's name.

Finally, our brave Perseus arrived at the island where he expected to see his dear mother. But during his absence, the wicked king had treated Danaë so very ill that she was compelled to make her escape, and had taken refuge in a temple, where some good old priests were extremely kind to her. These praiseworthy priests and the kind-hearted fisherman, who had first shown hospitality to Danaë and little Perseus when he found them afloat in the chest, seem to have been the only persons on the island who cared about doing right. All the rest of the people, as well as King Polydectes himself, were remarkably ill behaved and deserved no better destiny than that which was now to happen.

Not finding his mother at home, Perseus went straight to the palace and was immediately ushered into the presence of the king. Polydectes was by no means rejoiced to see him, for he had felt almost certain, in his own evil mind, that the Gorgons would have torn the poor young man to pieces and have eaten him up out of the way. However, seeing him safely returned, he put the best face he could upon the matter and asked Perseus how he had succeeded.

"Have you performed your promise?" inquired he. "Have you brought me the head of Medusa with the snaky locks? If not, young man, it will cost you dear; for I must have a bridal present for the beautiful Princess Hippodamia and there is nothing else that she would admire so much."

"Yes, please your Majesty," answered Perseus, in a quiet way, as if it were no very wonderful deed for such a young man as he to perform. "I have brought you the Gorgon's head, snaky locks and all!"

"Indeed! Pray, let me see it," quoth King Polydectes. "It must be a very curious spectacle if all that travelers tell it be true!"

"Your Majesty is in the right," replied Perseus. "It is really an object that will be pretty certain to fix the regards of all who look at it. And if your Majesty think fit, I would suggest that a holiday be proclaimed and that all your Majesty's subjects be summoned to behold this wonderful curiosity. Few of them, I imagine, have seen a Gorgon's head before and perhaps never may again!"

The king well knew that his subjects were an idle set of reprobates and very fond of sight-seeing, as idle persons usually are. So he took the young man's advice and sent out heralds and messengers in all directions to blow the trumpet at the street corners and in the market places and wherever two roads met, and summon everybody to court. Thither, accordingly, came a great multitude of good-for-nothing vagabonds, all of whom, out of pure love of mischief, would have been glad if Perseus had met with some ill-hap in his encounter with the Gorgons. If there were any better people in the island (as I really hope there may have been, although the story tells nothing about any such), they stayed quietly at home, minding their business and taking care of their little children. Most of the inhabitants, at all events, ran as fast as they could to the palace and shoved and pushed and elbowed one another in their eagerness to get near a balcony on which Perseus showed himself, holding the embroidered wallet in his hand.

On a platform within full view of the balcony sat the mighty King Polydectes, amid his evil counselors, and with his flattering courtiers in a semi-circle round about him. Monarch, counselors, courtiers and subjects all gazed eagerly toward Perseus.

"Show us the head! Show us the head!" shouted the people; and there was a fierceness in their cry as if they would tear Perseus to pieces unless he should satisfy them with what he had to show. "Show us the head of Medusa with the snaky locks!"

A feeling of sorrow and pity came over the youthful Perseus.

"O King Polydectes," cried he, "and ye many people, I am very loath to show you the Gorgon's head!"

"Ah, the villain and coward!" yelled the people more fiercely than before. "He is making game of us! He has no Gorgon's head! Show us the head if you have it, or we will take your own head for a football!"

The evil counselors whispered bad advice in the king's ear; the courtiers murmured, with one consent, that Perseus had shown disrespect to their royal lord and master; and the great King Polydectes himself waved his hand and ordered him, with the stern, deep voice of authority, on his peril, to produce the head.

"Show me the Gorgon's head or I will cut off your own!"

And Perseus sighed.

"This instant," repeated Polydectes, "or you die!"

"Behold it then!" cried Perseus in a voice like the blast of a trumpet.

And suddenly holding up the head, not an eyelid had time to wink before the wicked King Polydectes, his evil counselors and all his fierce subjects were no longer anything but the mere images of a monarch and his people. They were all fixed forever in the look and attitude of that moment! At the first glimpse of the terrible head of Medusa, they whitened into marble! And Perseus thrust the head back into his wallet and went to tell his dear mother that she need no longer be afraid of the wicked King Polydectes.

The Golden Fleece

When Jason, the son of the dethroned King of Iolchos, was a little boy, he was sent away from his parents and placed under the queerest schoolmaster that ever you heard of. This learned person was one of the people, or quadrupeds, called Centaurs. He lived in a cavern, and had the body and legs of a white horse, with the head and shoulders of a man. His name was Chiron; and in spite of his odd appearance, he was a very excellent teacher and had several scholars who afterward did him credit by making a great figure in the world. The famous Hercules was one, and so was Achilles, and Philoctetes likewise, and Æsculapius, who acquired immense repute as a doctor. The good Chiron taught his pupils how to play upon the harp, and how to cure diseases, and how to use the sword and shield, together with various other branches of education in which the lads of those days used to be instructed instead of writing and arithmetic.

I have sometimes suspected that Master Chiron was not really very different from other people, but that, being a kind-hearted and merry old fellow, he was in the habit of making believe that he was a horse, and scrambling about the schoolroom on all fours and letting the little boys ride upon his back. And so, when his scholars had grown up and grown old and were trotting their grandchildren on their knees, they told them about the sports of their school-days; and these young folks took the idea that their grandfathers had been taught their letters by a Centaur, half man and half horse. Little children, not quite understanding what is said to them, often get such absurd notions into their heads, you know.

Be that as it may, it has always been told for a fact (and always will be told, as long as the world lasts) that Chiron, with the head of a schoolmaster, had the body and legs of a horse. Just imagine the grave old gentleman clattering and stamping into the schoolroom on his four hoofs, perhaps treading on some little fellow's toes, flourishing his switch tail instead of a rod and now and then trotting out of doors to eat a mouthful of grass! I wonder what the blacksmith charged him for a set of iron shoes.

So Jason dwelt in the cave, with this four-footed Chiron from the time that he was an infant only a few months old, until he had grown to the full height of a man. He became a very good harper, I suppose, and skilful in the use of weapons and tolerably acquainted with herbs and other doctor's stuff, and above all, an admirable horseman; for, in teaching young people to ride, the good Chiron must have been without a rival among schoolmasters. At length, being now a tall and athletic youth, Jason resolved to seek his fortune in the world without asking Chiron's advice or telling him anything about the matter. This was very unwise, to be sure; and I hope none of you, my little hearers, will ever follow Jason's example. But, you are to understand, he had heard how that he himself was a prince royal, and how his father, King Æson, had been deprived of the kingdom of Iolchos by a certain Pelias, who would also have killed Jason had he not been hidden in the Centaur's cave. And being come to the strength of a man, Jason determined to set all this business to rights and to punish the wicked Pelias for wronging his dear father, and to cast him down from the throne and seat himself there instead.

With this intention he took a spear in each hand and threw a leopard's skin over his shoulders to keep off the rain, and set forth on his travels, with his long yellow ringlets waving in the wind. The part of his dress on which he most prided himself was a pair of sandals that had been his father's. They were handsomely embroidered and were tied upon his feet with strings of gold. But his whole attire was such as people did not very often see; and as he passed along, the women and children ran to the doors and windows, wondering whither this beautiful youth was journeying, with his leopard's skin and his golden-tied sandals, and what heroic deeds he meant to perform, with a spear in his right hand and another in his left.

I know not how far Jason had traveled when he came to a turbulent river, which rushed right across his pathway with specks of white foam along its black eddies, hurrying tumultuously onward and roaring angrily as it went. Though not a very broad river in the dry seasons of the year, it was now swollen by heavy rains and by the melting of the snow on the sides of Mount Olympus; and it thundered so loudly and looked so wild and dangerous that Jason, bold as he was, thought it prudent to pause upon the brink. The bed of the stream seemed to be strewn with sharp and rugged rocks, some of which thrust themselves above the water. By and by an uprooted tree, with shattered branches, came drifting along the current and got entangled among the rocks. Now and then a drowned sheep and once the carcass of a cow floated past.

In short, the swollen river had already done a great deal of mischief. It was evidently too deep for Jason to wade and too boisterous for him to swim; he could see no bridge, and as for a boat, had there been any, the rocks would have broken it to pieces in an instant.

"See the poor lad," said a cracked voice close to his side. "He must have had but a poor education, since he does not know how to cross a little stream like this. Or is he afraid of wetting his fine golden-stringed sandals? It is a pity his four-footed schoolmaster is not here to carry him safely across on his back!"

Jason looked round greatly surprised, for he did not know that anybody was near. But beside him stood an old woman, with a ragged mantle over her head, leaning on a staff, the top of which was carved into the shape of a cuckoo. She looked very aged and wrinkled and infirm; and yet her eyes, which were as brown as those of an ox, were so extremely large and beautiful that when they were fixed on Jason's eyes he could see nothing else but them. The old woman had a pomegranate in her hand, although the fruit was then quite out of season.

"Whither are you going, Jason?" she now asked.

She seemed to know his name, you will observe; and, indeed, those great brown eyes looked as if they had a knowledge of everything, whether past or to come. While Jason was gazing at her a peacock strutted forward and took his stand at the old woman's side.

"I am going to Iolchos," answered the young man, "to bid the wicked King Pelias come down from my father's throne and let me reign in his stead."

"Ah, well, then," said the old woman, still with the same cracked voice, "if that is all your business, you need not be in a very great hurry. Just take me on your back, there's a good youth, and carry me across the river. I and my peacock have something to do on the other side, as well as yourself."

"Good mother," replied Jason, "your business can hardly be so important as the pulling down a king from his throne. Besides, as you may see for yourself, the river is very boisterous; and if I should chance to stumble, it would sweep both of us away more easily than it has carried off yonder uprooted tree. I would gladly help you if I could, but I doubt whether I am strong enough to carry you across."

"Then," said she very scornfully, "neither are you strong enough to pull King Pelias off his throne. And, Jason, unless you will help an old woman at her need, you ought not to be a king. What are kings made for, save to succor the feeble and distressed? But do as you please. Either take me on your back, or with my poor old limbs I shall try my best to struggle across the stream."

Saying this, the old woman poked with her staff in the river as if to find the safest place in its rocky bed where she might make the first step. But Jason by this time had grown ashamed of his reluctance to help her. He felt that he could never forgive himself if this poor feeble creature should come to any harm in attempting to wrestle against the headlong current. The good Chiron, whether half horse or no, had taught him that the noblest use of his strength was to assist the weak; and also that he must treat every young woman as if she were his sister and every old one like a mother. Remembering these maxims, the vigorous and beautiful young man knelt down and requested the good dame to mount upon his back.

"The passage seems to me not very safe," he remarked, "but as your business is so urgent I will try to carry you across. If the river sweeps you away it shall take me, too."

"That, no doubt, will be a great comfort to both of us," quoth the old woman. "But never fear! We shall get safely across."

So she threw her arms around Jason's neck; and, lifting her from the ground, he stepped boldly into the raging and foamy current, and began to stagger away from the shore. As for the peacock, it alighted on the old dame's shoulder. Jason's two spears, one in each hand, kept him from stumbling and enabled him to feel his way among the hidden rocks; although every instant he expected that his companion and himself would go down the stream together with the driftwood of shattered trees and the carcasses of the sheep and cow. Down came the cold, snowy torrent from the steep side of Olympus, raging and thundering as if it had a real spite against Jason or, at all events, were determined to snatch off his living burden from his shoulders. When he was half way across the uprooted tree (which I have already told you about) broke loose from among the rocks and bore down upon him with all its splintered branches sticking out like the hundred arms of the giant Briareus. It rushed past, however, without touching him. But the next moment his foot was caught in a crevice between two rocks and stuck there so fast that in the effort to get free he lost one of his golden-stringed sandals.

At this accident Jason could not help uttering a cry of vexation.

"What is the matter, Jason?" asked the old woman.

"Matter enough," said the young man. "I have lost a sandal here among the rocks. And what sort of a figure shall I cut at the court of King Pelias with a golden-stringed sandal on one foot and the other foot bare!"

"Do not take it to heart," answered his companion cheerily. "You never met with better fortune than in losing that sandal. It satisfies me that you are the very person whom the Speaking Oak has been talking about."

There was no time just then to inquire what the Speaking Oak had said. But the briskness of her tone encouraged the young man; and, besides, he had never in his life felt so vigorous and mighty as since taking this old woman on his back. Instead of being exhausted he gathered strength as he went on; and, struggling up against the torrent, he at last gained the opposite shore, clambered up the bank and set down the old dame and her peacock safely on the grass. As soon as this was done, however, he could not help looking rather despondently at his bare foot, with only a remnant of the golden string of the sandal clinging round his ankle.

"You will get a handsomer pair of sandals by and by," said the old woman, with a kindly look out of her beautiful brown eyes. "Only let King Pelias get a glimpse of that bare foot and you shall see him turn as pale as ashes, I promise you. There is your path. Go along, my good Jason, and my blessing go with you. And when you sit on your throne remember the old woman whom you helped over the river."

With these words she hobbled away, giving him a smile over her shoulder as she departed. Whether the light of her beautiful brown eyes threw a glory round about her, or whatever the cause might be, Jason fancied that there was something very noble and majestic in her figure after all, and that, though her gait seemed to be a rheumatic hobble, yet she moved with as much grace and dignity as any queen on earth. Her peacock, which had now fluttered down from her shoulder, strutted behind her in prodigious pomp and spread out its magnificent tail on purpose for Jason to admire it.

When the old dame and her peacock were out of sight Jason set forward on his journey. After traveling a pretty long distance he came to a town situated at the foot of a mountain and not a great way from the shore of the sea. On the outside of the town there was an immense crowd of people, not only men and women, but children, too, all in their best clothes and evidently enjoying a holiday. The crowd was thickest toward the seashore, and in that direction, over the people's heads, Jason saw a wreath of smoke curling upward to the blue sky. He inquired of one of the multitude what town it was near by and why so many persons were here assembled together.

"This is the kingdom of Iolchos," answered the man, "and we are the subjects of King Pelias. Our monarch has summoned us together, that we may see him sacrifice a black bull to Neptune, who, they say, is his majesty's father. Yonder is the king, where you see the smoke going up from the altar."

While the man spoke he eyed Jason with great curiosity; for his garb was quite unlike that of the Iolchians, and it looked very odd to see a youth with a leopard's skin over his shoulders and each hand grasping a spear. Jason perceived, too, that the man stared particularly at his feet, one of which, you remember, was bare, while the other was decorated with his father's golden-stringed sandal.

"Look at him! only look at him!" said the man to his next neighbor. "Do you see? He wears but one sandal!"

Upon this, first one person and then another began to stare at Jason, and everybody seemed to be greatly struck with something in his aspect; though they turned their eyes much oftener toward his feet than to any other part of his figure. Besides, he could hear them whispering to one another.

"One sandal! One sandal!" they kept saying. "The man with one sandal! Here he is at last! Whence has he come? What does he mean to do? What will the king say to the one-sandaled man?"

Poor Jason was greatly abashed and made up his mind that the people of Iolchos were exceedingly ill-bred to take such public notice of an accidental deficiency in his dress.

Meanwhile, whether it were that they hustled him forward or that Jason of his own accord thrust a passage through the crowd, it so happened that he soon found himself close to the smoking altar, where King Pelias was sacrificing the black bull. The murmur and hum of the multitude, in their surprise at the spectacle of Jason with his one bare foot, grew so loud that it disturbed the ceremonies; and the king, holding the great knife with which he was just going to cut the bull's throat, turned angrily about and fixed his eyes on Jason. The people had now withdrawn from around him, so that the youth stood in an open space, near the smoking altar, front to front with the angry King Pelias.

"Who are you?" cried the king, with a terrible frown. "And how dare you make this disturbance, while I am sacrificing a black bull to my father Neptune?"

"It is no fault of mine," answered Jason. "Your majesty must blame the rudeness of your subjects, who have raised all this tumult because one of my feet happens to be bare."

When Jason said this the king gave a quick, startled glance at his feet.

"Ha!" muttered he, "here is the one-sandaled fellow, sure enough! What can I do with him?"

And he clutched more closely the great knife in his hand, as if he were half a mind to slay Jason instead of the black bull. The people round about caught up the king's words, indistinctly as they were uttered; and first there was a murmur among them and then a loud shout.

"The one-sandaled man has come! The prophecy must be fulfilled!"

For you are to know that many years before King Pelias had been told by the Speaking Oak of Dodona that a man with one sandal should cast him down from his throne. On this account he had given strict orders that nobody should ever come into his presence unless both sandals were securely tied upon his feet; and he kept an officer in his palace whose sole business it was to examine people's sandals and to supply them with a new pair at the expense of the royal treasury as soon as the old ones began to wear out. In the whole course of the king's reign he had never been thrown into such a fright and agitation as by the spectacle of poor Jason's bare foot. But as he was naturally a bold and hard-hearted man, he soon took courage and began to consider in what way he might rid himself of this terrible one-sandaled stranger.

"My good young man," said King Pelias, taking the softest tone imaginable in order to throw Jason off his guard, "you are excessively welcome to my kingdom. Judging by your dress, you must have traveled a long distance, for it is not the fashion to wear leopard-skins in this part of the world. Pray, what may I call your name, and where did you receive your education?"

"My name is Jason," answered the young stranger. "Ever since my infancy I have dwelt in the cave of Chiron the Centaur. He was my instructor, and taught me music and horsemanship and how to cure wounds, and likewise how to inflict wounds with my weapons!"

"I have heard of Chiron the schoolmaster," replied King Pelias, "and how that there is an immense deal of learning and wisdom in his head, although it happens to be set on a horse's body. It gives me great delight to see one of his scholars at my court. But to test how much you have profited under so excellent a teacher, will you allow me to ask you a single question?"

"I do not pretend to be very wise," said Jason; "but ask me what you please and I will answer to the best of my ability."

Now King Pelias meant cunningly to entrap the young man and to make him say something that should be the cause of mischief and destruction to himself. So with a crafty and evil smile upon his face, he spoke as follows:

"What would you do, brave Jason," asked he, "if there were a man in the world by whom, as you had reason to believe, you were doomed to be ruined and slain—what would you do, I say, if that man stood before you and in your power?"

When Jason saw the malice and wickedness which King Pelias could not prevent from gleaming out of his eyes, he probably guessed that the king had discovered what he came for, and that he intended to turn his own words against himself. Still, he scorned to tell a falsehood. Like an upright and honorable prince, as he was, he determined to speak out the real truth. Since the king had chosen to ask him the question and since Jason had promised him an answer, there was no right way save to tell him precisely what would be the most prudent thing to do if he had his worst enemy in his power.

Therefore, after a moment's consideration, he spoke up with a firm and manly voice:

"I would send such a man," said he, "in quest of the Golden Fleece!"

This enterprise, you will understand, was, of all others, the most difficult and dangerous in the world. In the first place, it would be necessary to make a long voyage through unknown seas. There was hardly a hope or a possibility that any young man who should undertake this voyage would either succeed in obtaining the Golden Fleece or would survive to return home and tell of the perils he had run. The eyes of King Pelias sparkled with joy, therefore, when he heard Jason's reply.

"Well said, wise man with the one sandal!" cried he. "Go, then, and at the peril of your life bring me back the Golden Fleece!"

"I go," answered Jason composedly. "If I fail, you need not fear that I will ever come back to trouble you again. But if I return to Iolchos with the prize, then, King Pelias, you must hasten down from your lofty throne and give me your crown and scepter."

"That I will," said the king, with a sneer. "Meantime I will keep them very safely for you."

The first thing that Jason thought of doing after he left the king's presence was to go to Dodona and inquire of the Talking Oak what course it was best to pursue. This wonderful tree stood in the center of an ancient wood. Its stately trunk rose up a hundred feet into the air and threw a broad and dense shadow over more than an acre of ground. Standing beneath it, Jason looked up among the knotted branches and green leaves and into the mysterious heart of the old tree, and spoke aloud, as if he were addressing some person who was hidden in the depths of the foliage.

"What shall I do," said he, "in order to win the Golden Fleece?"

At first there was a deep silence, not only within the shadow of the Talking Oak, but all through the solitary wood. In a moment or two, however, the leaves of the oak began to stir and rustle as if a gentle breeze were wandering among them, although the other trees of the wood were perfectly still. The sound grew louder and became like the roar of a high wind. By and by Jason imagined that he could distinguish words, but very confusedly, because each separate leaf of the tree seemed to be a tongue and the whole myriad of tongues were babbling at once. But the noise waxed broader and deeper until it resembled a tornado sweeping through the oak and making one great utterance out of the thousand and thousand of little murmurs which each leafy tongue had caused by its rustling. And now, though it still had the tone of a mighty wind roaring among the branches, it was also like a deep bass voice speaking, as distinctly as a tree could be expected to speak, the following words:

"Go to Argus, the shipbuilder, and bid him build a galley with fifty oars."

Then the voice melted again into the indistinct murmur of the rustling leaves and died gradually away. When it was quite gone Jason felt inclined to doubt whether he had actually heard the words or whether his fancy had not shaped them out of the ordinary sound made by a breeze while passing through the thick foliage of the tree.

But on inquiry among the people of Iolchos, he found that there was really a man in the city by the name of Argus, who was a very skilful builder of vessels. This showed some intelligence in the oak, else how should it have known that any such person existed? At Jason's request Argus readily consented to build him a galley so big that it should require fifty strong men to row it, although no vessel of such a size and burden had heretofore been seen in the world. So the head carpenter and all his journeymen and apprentices began their work; and for a good while afterward there they were busily employed hewing out the timbers and making a great clatter with their hammers, until the new ship, which was called the Argo, seemed to be quite ready for sea. And as the Talking Oak had already given him such good advice, Jason thought that it would not be amiss to ask for a little more. He visited it again, therefore, and standing beside its huge, rough trunk, inquired what he should do next.

This time there was no such universal quivering of the leaves throughout the whole tree as there had been before. But after a while Jason observed that the foliage of a great branch which stretched above his head had begun to rustle as if the wind were stirring that one bough, while all the other boughs of the oak were at rest.

"Cut me off!" said the branch, as soon as it could speak distinctly; "cut me off! cut me off! and carve me into a figurehead for your galley."

Accordingly, Jason took the branch at its word and lopped it off the tree. A carver in the neighborhood engaged to make the figurehead. He was a tolerably good workman and had already carved several figureheads in what he intended for feminine shapes, and looking pretty much like those which we see nowadays stuck up under a vessel's bowsprit, with great staring eyes that never wink at the dash of the spray. But (what was very strange) the carver found that his hand was guided by some unseen power and by a skill beyond his own, and that his tools shaped out an image which he had never dreamed of. When the work was finished it turned out to be the figure of a beautiful woman, with a helmet on her head, from beneath which the long ringlets fell down upon her shoulders. On the left arm was a shield and in its center appeared a lifelike representation of the head of Medusa with the snaky locks. The right arm was extended as if pointing onward. The face of this wonderful statue, though not angry or forbidding, was so grave and majestic that perhaps you might call it severe; and as for the mouth, it seemed just ready to unclose its lips and utter words of the deepest wisdom.

Jason was delighted with the oaken image and gave the carver no rest until it was completed and set up where a figurehead has always stood, from that time to this, in the vessel's prow.

"And now," cried he, as he stood gazing at the calm, majestic face of the statue, "I must go to the Talking Oak and inquire what next to do."

"There is no need of that, Jason," said a voice which, though it was far lower, reminded him of the mighty tones of the great oak. "When you desire good advice you can seek it of me."

Jason had been looking straight into the face of the image when these words were spoken. But he could hardly believe either his ears or his eyes. The truth was, however, that the oaken lips had moved, and to all appearance, the voice had proceeded from the statue's mouth. Recovering a little from his surprise, Jason bethought himself that the image had been carved out of the wood of the Talking Oak, and that, therefore, it was really no great wonder, but, on the contrary, the most natural thing in the world, that it should possess the faculty of speech. It should have been very odd indeed if it had not. But certainly it was a great piece of good fortune that he should be able to carry so wise a block of wood along with him in his perilous voyage.

"Tell me, wondrous image," exclaimed Jason, "since you inherit the wisdom of the Speaking Oak of Dodona, whose daughter you are—tell me, where shall I find fifty bold youths who will take each of them an oar of my galley? They must have sturdy arms to row and brave hearts to encounter perils, or we shall never win the Golden Fleece."

"Go," replied the oaken image, "go, summon all the heroes of Greece."

And, in fact, considering what a great deed was to be done, could any advice be wiser than this which Jason received from the figurehead of his vessel? He lost no time in sending messengers to all the cities, and making known to the whole people of Greece that Prince Jason, the son of King Æson, was going in quest of the Fleece of Gold, and he desired the help of forty-nine of the bravest and strongest young men alive, to row his vessel and share his dangers. And Jason himself would be the fiftieth.

At this news the adventurous youths all over the country began to bestir themselves. Some of them had already fought with giants and slain dragons; and the younger ones, who had not yet met with such good fortune, thought it a shame to have lived so long without getting astride of a flying serpent or sticking their spears into a Chimæra, or at least thrusting their right arms down a monstrous lion's throat. There was a fair prospect that they would meet with plenty of such adventures before finding the Golden Fleece. As soon as they could furbish up their helmets and shields, therefore, and gird on their trusty swords, they came thronging to Iolchos and clambered on board the new galley. Shaking hands with Jason, they assured him that they did not care a pin for their lives, but would help row the vessel to the remotest edge of the world and as much further as he might think it best to go.

Many of these brave fellows had been educated by Chiron, the four-footed pedagogue, and were therefore old schoolmates of Jason and knew him to be a lad of spirit. The mighty Hercules, whose shoulders afterward held up the sky, was one of them. And there were Castor and Pollux, the twin brothers, who were never accused of being chicken-hearted, although they had been hatched out of an egg; and Theseus, who was so renowned for killing the Minotaur; and Lynceus, with his wonderfully sharp eyes, which could see through a millstone or look right down into the depths of the earth and discover the treasures that were there; and Orpheus, the very best of harpers, who sang and played upon his lyre so sweetly that the brute beasts stood upon their hind legs and capered merrily to the music. Yes, and at some of his more moving tunes the rocks bestirred their moss-grown bulk out of the ground, and a grove of forest trees uprooted themselves and, nodding their tops to one another, performed a country dance.

One of the rowers was a beautiful young woman named Atalanta, who had been nursed among the mountains by a bear. So light of foot was this fair damsel that she could step from one foamy crest of a wave to the foamy crest of another without wetting more than the sole of her sandal. She had grown up in a very wild way and talked much about the rights of women, and loved hunting and war far better than her needle. But in my opinion, the most remarkable of this famous company were two sons of the North Wind (airy youngsters, and of rather a blustering disposition), who had wings on their shoulders, and, in case of a calm, could puff out their cheeks and blow almost as fresh a breeze as their father. I ought not to forget the prophets and conjurers, of whom there were several in the crew, and who could foretell what would happen tomorrow, or the next day, or a hundred years hence, but were generally quite unconscious of what was passing at the moment.

Jason appointed Tiphys to be helmsman, because he was a star-gazer and knew the points of the compass. Lynceus, on account of his sharp sight, was stationed as a lookout in the prow, where he saw a whole day's sail ahead, but was rather apt to overlook things that lay directly under his nose. If the sea only happened to be deep enough, however, Lynceus could tell you exactly what kind of rocks or sands were at the bottom of it; and he often cried out to his companions that they were sailing over heaps of sunken treasure, which yet he was none the richer for beholding. To confess the truth, few people believed him when he said it.

Well! But when the Argonauts, as these fifty brave adventurers were called, had prepared everything for the voyage, an unforeseen difficulty threatened to end it before it was begun. The vessel, you must understand, was so long and broad and ponderous that the united force of all the fifty was insufficient to shove her into the water. Hercules, I suppose, had not grown to his full strength, else he might have set her afloat as easily as a little boy launches his boat upon a puddle. But here were these fifty heroes, pushing and straining and growing red in the face without making the Argo start an inch. At last, quite wearied out, they sat themselves down on the shore, exceedingly disconsolate and thinking that the vessel must be left to rot and fall in pieces and that they must either swim across the sea or lose the Golden Fleece.

All at once Jason bethought himself of the galley's miraculous figurehead.

"Oh, daughter of the Talking Oak," cried he, "how shall we set to work to get our vessel into the water?"

"Seat yourselves," answered the image (for it had known what had ought to be done from the very first and was only waiting for the question to be put), "seat yourselves and handle your oars, and let Orpheus play upon his harp."

Immediately the fifty heroes got on board, and seizing their oars, held them perpendicularly in the air, while Orpheus (who liked such a task far better than rowing) swept his fingers across the harp. At the first ringing note of the music they felt the vessel stir. Orpheus thrummed away briskly and the galley slid at once into the sea, dipping her prow so deeply that the figurehead drank the wave with its marvelous lips, and rising again as buoyant as a swan. The rowers plied their fifty oars, the white foam boiled up before the prow, the water gurgled and bubbled in their wake, while Orpheus continued to play so lively a strain of music that the vessel seemed to dance over the billows by way of keeping time to it. Thus triumphantly did the Argo sail out of the harbor amid the huzzas and good wishes of everybody except the wicked old Pelias, who stood on a promontory scowling at her and wishing that he could blow out of his lungs the tempest of wrath that was in his heart and so sink the galley with all on board. When they had sailed above fifty miles over the sea Lynceus happened to cast his sharp eyes behind, and said that there was this bad-hearted king, still perched upon the promontory, and scowling so gloomily that it looked like a black thunder-cloud in that quarter of the horizon.

In order to make the time pass away more pleasantly during the voyage, the heroes talked about the Golden Fleece. It originally belonged, it appears, to a Bœotian ram, who had taken on his back two children, when in danger of their lives, and fled with them over land and sea as far as Colchis. One of the children, whose name was Helle, fell into the sea and was drowned. But the other (a little boy named Phrixus) was brought safe ashore by the faithful ram, who, however, was so exhausted that he immediately lay down and died. In memory of this good deed, and as a token of his true heart, the fleece of the poor dead ram was miraculously changed to gold and became one of the most beautiful objects ever seen on earth. It was hung upon a tree in a sacred grove, where it had now been kept I know not how many years, and was the envy of mighty kings who had nothing so magnificent in any of their palaces.

If I were to tell you all the adventures of the Argonauts it would take me till nightfall and perhaps a great deal longer. There was no lack of wonderful events, as you may judge from what you have already heard. At a certain island they were hospitably received by King Cyzicus, its sovereign, who made a feast for them and treated them like brothers. But the Argonauts saw that this good king looked downcast and very much troubled, and they therefore inquired of him what was the matter. King Cyzicus hereupon informed them that he and his subjects were greatly abused and incommoded by the inhabitants of a neighboring mountain, who made war upon them and killed many people and ravaged the country. And while they were talking about it Cyzicus pointed to the mountain and asked Jason and his companions what they saw there.

"I see some very tall objects," answered Jason, "but they are at such a distance that I cannot distinctly make out what they are. To tell your majesty the truth, they look so very strangely that I am inclined to think them clouds which have chanced to take something like human shapes."

"I see them very plainly," remarked Lynceus, whose eyes, you know, were as far-sighted as a telescope. "They are a band of enormous giants, all of whom have six arms apiece, and a club, a sword or some other weapon in each of their hands."

"You have excellent eyes," said King Cyzicus. "Yes, they are six-armed giants, as you say, and these are the enemies whom I and my subjects have to contend with."

The next day, when the Argonauts were about setting sail, down came these terrible giants, stepping a hundred yards at a stride, brandishing their six arms apiece and looking very formidable so far aloft in the air. Each of these monsters was able to carry on a whole war by himself, for with one of his arms he could fling immense stones and wield a club with another and a sword with a third, while a fourth was poking a long spear at the enemy and the fifth and sixth were shooting him with a bow and arrow. But luckily, though the giants were so huge and had so many arms, they had each but one heart and that no bigger nor braver than the heart of an ordinary man. Besides, if they had been like the hundred-armed Briareus, the brave Argonauts would have given them their hands full of fight. Jason and his friends went boldly to meet them, slew a great many and made the rest take to their heels—so that if the giants had had six legs apiece instead of six arms, it would have served them better to run away with.

Another strange adventure happened when the voyagers came to Thrace, where they found a poor blind king named Phineus, deserted by his subjects and living in a very sorrowful way all by himself. On Jason's inquiring whether they could do him any service, the king answered that he was terribly tormented by three great winged creatures called Harpies, which had the faces of women and the wings, bodies and claws of vultures. These ugly wretches were in the habit of snatching away his dinner, and allowed him no peace of his life. Upon hearing this the Argonauts spread a plentiful feast on the seashore, well knowing from what the blind king said of their greediness that the Harpies would snuff up the scent of the victuals and quickly come to steal them away. And so it turned out, for hardly was the table set before the three hideous vulture-women came flapping their wings, seized the food in their talons and flew off as fast as they could. But the two sons of the North Wind drew their swords, spread their pinions and set off through the air in pursuit of the thieves, whom they at last overtook among some islands, after a chase of hundreds of miles. The two winged youths blustered terribly at the Harpies (for they had the rough temper of their father), and so frightened them with their drawn swords that they solemnly promised never to trouble King Phineus again.

Then the Argonauts sailed onward and met with many other marvelous incidents, any one of which would make a story by itself. At one time they landed on an island and were reposing on the grass, when they suddenly found themselves assailed by what seemed a shower of steel-headed arrows. Some of them stuck in the ground, while others hit against their shields and several penetrated their flesh. The fifty heroes started up and looked about them for the hidden enemy, but could find none nor see any spot on the whole island where even a single archer could lie concealed. Still, however, the steel-headed arrows came whizzing among them; and at last, happening to look upward, they beheld a large flock of birds hovering and wheeling aloft and shooting their feathers down upon the Argonauts. These feathers were the steel-headed arrows that had so tormented them. There was no possibility of making any resistance, and the fifty heroic Argonauts might all have been killed or wounded by a flock of troublesome birds without ever setting eyes on the Golden Fleece if Jason had not thought of asking the advice of the oaken image.

So he ran to the galley as fast as his legs would carry him.

"O daughter of the Speaking Oak," cried he, all out of breath, "we need your wisdom more than ever before! We are in great peril from a flock of birds, who are shooting us with their steel-pointed feathers. What can we do to drive them away?"

"Make a clatter on your shields," said the image.

On receiving this excellent counsel, Jason hurried back to his companions (who were far more dismayed than when they fought with the six-armed giants) and bade them strike with their swords upon their brazen shields. Forthwith the fifty heroes set heartily to work, banging with might and main, and raised such a terrible clatter that the birds made what haste they could to get away; and though they had shot half the feathers out of their wings, they were soon seen skimming among the clouds, a long distance off and looking like a flock of wild geese. Orpheus celebrated this victory by playing a triumphant anthem on his harp, and sang so melodiously that Jason begged him to desist, lest, as the steel-feathered birds had been driven away by an ugly sound, they might be enticed back again by a sweet one.

While the Argonauts remained on this island they saw a small vessel approaching the shore, in which were two young men of princely demeanor, and exceedingly handsome, as young princes generally were in those days. Now, who do you imagine these two voyagers turned out to be? Why, if you will believe me, they were the sons of that very Phrixus, who in his childhood had been carried to Colchis on the back of the golden-fleeced ram. Since that time Phrixus had married the king's daughter, and the two young princes had been born and brought up at Colchis, and had spent their play days on the outskirts of the grove, in the center of which the Golden Fleece was hanging upon a tree. They were now on their way to Greece, in hopes of getting back a kingdom that had been wrongfully taken from their father.

When the princes understood whither the Argonauts were going they offered to turn back and guide them to Colchis. At the same time, however, they spoke as if it were very doubtful whether Jason would succeed in getting the Golden Fleece. According to their account, the tree on which it hung was guarded by a terrible dragon, who never failed to devour at one mouthful every person who might venture within his reach.

"There are other difficulties in the way," continued the young princes. "But is not this enough? Ah, brave Jason, turn back before it is too late! It would grieve us to the heart if you and your forty-nine brave companions should be eaten up, at fifty mouthfuls, by this execrable dragon."

"My young friends," quietly replied Jason, "I do not wonder that you think the dragon very terrible. You have grown up from infancy in the fear of this monster, and therefore still regard him with the awe that children feel for the bugbears and hobgoblins which their nurses have talked to them about. But in my view of the matter, the dragon is merely a pretty large serpent who is not half so likely to snap me up at one mouthful as I am to cut off his ugly head and strip the skin from his body. At all events, turn back who may, I will never see Greece again unless I carry with me the Golden Fleece."

"We will none of us turn back!" cried his forty-nine brave comrades. "Let us get on board the galley this instant, and if the dragon is to make a breakfast of us, much good may it do him."

And Orpheus (whose custom it was to set everything to music) began to harp and sing most gloriously, and made every mother's son of them feel as if nothing in this world were so delectable as to fight dragons and nothing so truly honorable as to be eaten up at one mouthful, in case of the worst.

After this (being now under the guidance of the two princes, who were well acquainted with the way) they quickly sailed to Colchis. When the king of the country, whose name was Æetes, heard of their arrival, he instantly summoned Jason to court. The king was a stern and cruel-looking potentate, and though he put on as polite and hospitable an expression as he could, Jason did not like his face a whit better than that of the wicked King Pelias, who dethroned his father.

"You are welcome, brave Jason," said King Æetes. "Pray, are you on a pleasure voyage?—or do you meditate the discovery of unknown islands?—or what other cause has procured me the happiness of seeing you at my court?"

"Great sir," replied Jason, with an obeisance—for Chiron had taught him how to behave with propriety, whether to kings or beggars—"I have come hither with a purpose which I now beg your majesty's permission to execute. King Pelias, who sits on my father's throne (to which he has no more right than to the one on which your excellent majesty is now seated), has engaged to come down from it and to give me his crown and scepter, provided I bring him the Golden Fleece. This, as your majesty is aware, is now hanging on a tree here at Colchis; and I humbly solicit your gracious leave to take it away."

In spite of himself, the king's face twisted itself into an angry frown; for, above all things else in the world, he prized the Golden Fleece, and was even suspected of having done a very wicked act in order to get it into his own possession. It put him into the worst possible humor, therefore, to hear that the gallant Prince Jason and forty-nine of the bravest young warriors of Greece had come to Colchis with the sole purpose of taking away his chief treasure.

"Do you know," asked King Æetes, eyeing Jason very sternly, "what are the conditions which you must fulfill before getting possession of the Golden Fleece?"

"I have heard," rejoined the youth, "that a dragon lies beneath the tree on which the prize hangs, and that whoever approaches him runs the risk of being devoured at a mouthful."

"True," said the king, with a smile that did not look particularly good-natured. "Very true, young man. But there are other things as hard, or perhaps a little harder, to be done before you can even have the privilege of being devoured by the dragon. For example, you must first tame my two brazen-footed and brazen-lunged bulls, which Vulcan, the wonderful blacksmith, made for me. There is a furnace in each of their stomachs, and they breathe such hot fire out of their mouths and nostrils that nobody has hitherto gone nigh them without being instantly burned to a small, black cinder. What do you think of this, my brave Jason?"

"I must encounter the peril," answered Jason composedly, "since it stands in the way of my purpose."

"After taming the fiery bulls," continued King Æetes, who was determined to scare Jason if possible, "you must yoke them to a plow and must plow the sacred earth in the grove of Mars and sow some of the same dragon's teeth from which Cadmus raised a crop of armed men. They are an unruly set of reprobates, those sons of the dragon's teeth, and unless you treat them suitably, they will fall upon you sword in hand. You and your forty-nine Argonauts, my bold Jason, are hardly numerous or strong enough to fight with such a host as will spring up."

"My master Chiron," replied Jason, "taught me long ago the story of Cadmus. Perhaps I can manage the quarrelsome sons of the dragon's teeth as well as Cadmus did."

"I wish the dragon had him," muttered King Æetes to himself, "and the four-footed pedant, his schoolmaster, into the bargain. Why, what a foolhardy, self-conceited coxcomb he is! We'll see what my fire-breathing bulls will do for him. Well, Prince Jason," he continued aloud, and as complacently as he could, "make yourself comfortable for today, and tomorrow morning, since you insist upon it, you shall try your skill at the plow."

While the king talked with Jason a beautiful young woman was standing behind the throne. She fixed her eyes earnestly upon the youthful stranger and listened attentively to every word that was spoken, and when Jason withdrew from the king's presence this young woman followed him out of the room.

"I am the king's daughter," she said to him, "and my name is Medea. I know a great deal of which other young princesses are ignorant and can do many things which they would be afraid so much as to dream of. If you will trust to me I can instruct you how to tame the fiery bulls and sow the dragon's teeth and get the Golden Fleece."

"Indeed, beautiful princess," answered Jason, "if you will do me this service I promise to be grateful to you my whole life long."

Gazing at Medea, he beheld a wonderful intelligence in her face. She was one of those persons whose eyes are full of mystery; so that while looking into them, you seem to see a very great way, as into a deep well, yet can never be certain whether you see into the furthest depths or whether there be not something else hidden at the bottom. If Jason had been capable of fearing anything he would have been afraid of making this young princess his enemy; for, beautiful as she now looked, she might the very next instant become as terrible as the dragon that kept watch over the Golden Fleece.

"Princess," he exclaimed, "you seem indeed very wise and very powerful. But how can you help me to do the things of which you speak? Are you an enchantress?"

"Yes, Prince Jason," answered Medea, with a smile, "you have hit upon the truth. I am an enchantress. Circe, my father's sister, taught me to be one, and I could tell you, if I pleased, who was the old woman with the peacock, the pomegranate and the cuckoo staff, whom you carried over the river; and likewise, who it is that speaks through the lips of the oaken image that stands in the prow of your galley. I am acquainted with some of your secrets, you perceive. It is well for you that I am favorably inclined, for otherwise you would hardly escape being snapped up by the dragon."

"I should not so much care for the dragon," replied Jason, "if I only knew how to manage the brazen-footed and fiery-lunged bulls."

"If you are as brave as I think you, and as you have need to be," said Medea, "your own bold heart will teach you that there is but one way of dealing with a mad bull. What it is I leave you to find out in the moment of peril. As for the fiery breath of these animals, I have a charmed ointment here which will prevent you from being burned up and cure you if you chance to be a little scorched."

So she put a golden box into his hand and directed him how to apply the perfumed unguent which it contained, and where to meet her at midnight.

"Only be brave," added she, "and before daybreak the brazen bulls shall be tamed."

The young man assured her that his heart would not fail him. He then rejoined his comrades, and told them what had passed between the princess and himself, and warned them to be in readiness in case there might be need of their help.

At the appointed hour he met the beautiful Medea on the marble steps of the king's palace. She gave him a basket, in which were the dragon's teeth, just as they had been pulled out of the monster's jaws by Cadmus long ago. Medea then led Jason down the palace steps and through the silent streets of the city and into the royal pasture-ground, where the two brazen-footed bulls were kept. It was a starry night, with a bright gleam along the eastern edge of the sky, where the moon was soon going to show herself. After entering the pasture the princess paused and looked around.

"There they are," said she, "reposing themselves and chewing their fiery cuds in that furthest corner of the field. It will be excellent sport, I assure you, when they catch a glimpse of your figure. My father and all his court delight in nothing so much as to see a stranger trying to yoke them in order to come at the Golden Fleece. It makes a holiday in Colchis whenever such a thing happens. For my part, I enjoy it immensely. You cannot imagine in what a mere twinkling of an eye their hot breath shrivels a young man into a black cinder."

"Are you sure, beautiful Medea," asked Jason, "quite sure, that the unguent in the gold box will prove a remedy against those terrible burns?"

"If you doubt, if you are in the least afraid," said the princess, looking him in the face by the dim starlight, "you had better never have been born than go a step nigher to the bulls."

But Jason had set his heart steadfastly on getting the Golden Fleece, and I positively doubt whether he would have gone back without it even had he been certain of finding himself turned into a red-hot cinder, or a handful of white ashes the instant he made a step further. He therefore let go Medea's hand and walked boldly forward in the direction whither she had pointed. At some distance before him he perceived four streams of fiery vapor, regularly appearing and again vanishing after dimly lighting up the surrounding obscurity. These, you will understand, were caused by the breath of the brazen bulls, which was quietly stealing out of their four nostrils as they lay chewing their cuds.

At the first two or three steps which Jason made the four fiery streams appeared to gush out somewhat more plentifully, for the two brazen bulls had heard his foot-tramp and were lifting up their hot noses to snuff the air. He went a little further, and by the way in which the red vapor now spouted forth he judged that the creatures had got upon their feet. Now he could see glowing sparks and vivid jets of flame. At the next step each of the bulls made the pasture echo with a terrible roar, while the burning breath which they thus belched forth lit up the whole field with a momentary flash.

One other stride did bold Jason make; and suddenly, as a streak of lightning, on came these fiery animals, roaring like thunder and sending out sheets of white flame, which so kindled up the scene that the young man could discern every object more distinctly than by daylight. Most distinctly of all he saw the two horrible creatures galloping right down upon him, their brazen hoofs rattling and ringing over the ground and their tails sticking up stiffly into the air, as has always been the fashion with angry bulls. Their breath scorched the herbage before them. So intensely hot it was, indeed, that it caught a dry tree under which Jason was now standing and set it all in a light blaze. But as for Jason himself (thanks to Medea's enchanted ointment), the white flame curled around his body without injuring him a jot more than if he had been made of asbestos.

Greatly encouraged at finding himself not yet turned into a cinder, the young man awaited the attack of the bulls. Just as the brazen brutes fancied themselves sure of tossing him into the air he caught one of them by the horn and the other by his screwed-up tail and held them in a grip like that of an iron vise, one with his right hand, the other with his left. Well, he must have been wonderfully strong in his arms, to be sure! But the secret of the matter was that the brazen bulls were enchanted creatures and that Jason had broken the spell of their fiery fierceness by his bold way of handling them. And ever since that time it has been the favorite method of brave men, when danger assails them, to do what they call "taking the bull by the horns"; and to grip him by the tail is pretty much the same thing—that is, to throw aside fear and overcome the peril by despising it.

It was now easy to yoke the bulls and to harness them to the plow which had lain rusting on the ground for a great many years gone by, so long was it before anybody could be found capable of plowing that piece of land. Jason, I suppose, had been taught how to draw a furrow by the good old Chiron, who, perhaps, used to allow himself to be harnessed to the plow. At any rate, our hero succeeded perfectly well in breaking up the greensward; and by the time that the moon was a quarter of her journey up the sky the plowed field lay before him, a large tract of black earth, ready to be sown with the dragon's teeth. So Jason scattered them broadcast and harrowed them into the soil with a brush-harrow, and took his stand on the edge of the field, anxious to see what would happen next.

"Must we wait long for harvest-time?" he inquired of Medea, who was now standing by his side.

"Whether sooner or later, it will be sure to come," answered the princess. "A crop of armed men never fails to spring up when the dragon's teeth have been sown."

The moon was now high aloft in the heavens and threw its bright beams over the plowed field, where as yet there was nothing to be seen. Any farmer, on viewing it, would have said that Jason must wait weeks before the green blades would peep from among the clods, and whole months before the yellow grain would be ripened for the sickle. But by and by, all over the field, there was something that glistened in the moonbeams like sparkling drops of dew. These bright objects sprouted higher and proved to be the steel heads of spears. Then there was a dazzling gleam from a vast number of polished brass helmets, beneath which, as they grew further out of the soil, appeared the dark and bearded visages of warriors, struggling to free themselves from the imprisoning earth. The first look that they gave at the upper world was a glare of wrath and defiance. Next were seen their bright breastplates; in every right hand there was a sword or a spear and on each left arm a shield; and when this strange crop of warriors had but half grown out of the earth, they struggled—such was their impatience of restraint—and, as it were, tore themselves up by the roots. Wherever a dragon's tooth had fallen, there stood a man armed for battle. They made a clangor with their swords against their shields, and eyed one another fiercely; for they had come into this beautiful world and into the peaceful moonlight full of rage and stormy passions and ready to take the life of every human brother in recompense for the boon of their own existence.

There have been many other armies in the world that seemed to possess the same fierce nature with the one which had now sprouted from the dragon's teeth; but these in the moonlit field were the more excusable, because they never had women for their mothers. And now it would have rejoiced any great captain who was bent on conquering the world, like Alexander or Napoleon, to raise a crop of armed soldiers as easily as Jason did!

For awhile the warriors stood flourishing their weapons, clashing their swords against their shields and boiling over with the red-hot thirst for battle. Then they began to shout, "Show us the enemy! Lead us to the charge! Death or victory! Come on, brave comrades! Conquer or die!" and a hundred other outcries, such as men always bellow forth on a battle-field and which these dragon people seemed to have at their tongues' ends. At last the front rank caught sight of Jason, who, beholding the flash of so many weapons in the moonlight, had thought it best to draw his sword. In a moment all the sons of the dragon's teeth appeared to take Jason for an enemy; and crying with one voice, "Guard the Golden Fleece!" they ran at him with uplifted swords and protruded spears. Jason knew that it would be impossible to withstand this bloodthirsty battalion with his single arm, but determined, since there was nothing better to be done, to die as valiantly as if he himself had sprung from a dragon's tooth.

Medea, however, bade him snatch up a stone from the ground.

"Throw it among them quickly!" cried she. "It is the only way to save yourself."

The armed men were now so nigh that Jason could discern the fire flashing out of their enraged eyes, when he let fly the stone and saw it strike the helmet of a tall warrior who was rushing upon him with his blade aloft. The stone glanced from this man's helmet to the shield of his nearest comrade, and thence flew right into the angry face of another, hitting him smartly between the eyes. Each of the three who had been struck by the stone took it for granted that his next neighbor had given him a blow; and instead of running any further toward Jason, they began to fight among themselves. The confusion spread through the host, so that it seemed scarcely a moment before they were all hacking, hewing and stabbing at one another, lopping off arms, heads and legs and doing such memorable deeds that Jason was filled with immense admiration; although, at the same time, he could not help laughing to behold these mighty men punishing each other for an offense which he himself had committed. In an incredibly short space of time (almost as short, indeed, as it had taken them to grow up) all but one of the heroes of the dragon's teeth were stretched lifeless on the field. The last survivor, the bravest and strongest of the whole, had just force enough to wave his crimson sword over his head and give a shout of exultation, crying, "Victory! Victory! Immortal fame!" when he himself fell down and lay quietly among his slain brethren.

And there was the end of the army that had sprouted from the dragon's teeth. That fierce and feverish fight was the only enjoyment which they had tasted on this beautiful earth.

"Let them sleep in the bed of honor," said the Princess Medea, with a sly smile at Jason. "The world will always have simpletons enough, just like them, fighting and dying for they know not what, and fancying that posterity will take the trouble to put laurel wreaths on their rusty and battered helmets. Could you help smiling, Prince Jason, to see the self-conceit of that last fellow, just as he tumbled down?"

"It made me very sad," answered Jason gravely. "And to tell you the truth, princess, the Golden Fleece does not appear so well worth the winning, after what I have here beheld."

"You will think differently in the morning," said Medea. "True, the Golden Fleece may not be so valuable as you have thought it; but then there is nothing better in the world, and one must needs have an object, you know. Come! Your night's work has been well performed; and tomorrow you can inform King Æetes that the first part of your allotted task is fulfilled."

Agreeably to Medea's advice, Jason went betimes in the morning to the palace of king Æetes. Entering the presence chamber, he stood at the foot of the throne and made a low obeisance.

"Your eyes look heavy, Prince Jason," observed the king; "you appear to have spent a sleepless night. I hope you have been considering the matter a little more wisely and have concluded not to get yourself scorched to a cinder in attempting to tame my brazen-lunged bulls."

"That is already accomplished, may it please your majesty," replied Jason. "The bulls have been tamed and yoked; the field has been plowed; the dragon's teeth have been sown broadcast and harrowed into the soil; the crop of armed warriors has sprung up and they have slain one another to the last man. And now I solicit your majesty's permission to encounter the dragon, that I may take down the Golden Fleece from the tree and depart with my forty-nine comrades."

King Æetes scowled and looked very angry and excessively disturbed; for he knew that, in accordance with his kingly promise, he ought now to permit Jason to win the fleece if his courage and skill should enable him to do so. But since the young man had met with such good luck in the matter of the brazen bulls and dragon's teeth, the king feared that he would be equally successful in slaying the dragon. And therefore, though he would gladly have seen Jason snapped up at a mouthful, he was resolved (and it was a very wrong thing of this wicked potentate) not to run any further risk of losing his beloved fleece.

"You never would have succeeded in this business, young man," said he, "if my undutiful daughter Medea had not helped you with her enchantments. Had you acted fairly, you would have been at this instant a black cinder or a handful of white ashes. I forbid you, on pain of death, to make any more attempts to get the Golden Fleece. To speak my mind plainly, you shall never set eyes on so much as one of its glistening locks."

Jason left the king's presence in great sorrow and anger. He could think of nothing better to be done than to summon together his forty-nine brave Argonauts, march at once to the grove of Mars, slay the dragon, take possession of the Golden Fleece, get on board the Argo and spread all sail for Iolchos. The success of this scheme depended, it is true, on the doubtful point whether all the fifty heroes might not be snapped up as so many mouthfuls by the dragon. But as Jason was hastening down the palace steps, the Princess Medea called after him and beckoned him to return. Her black eyes shone upon him with such a keen intelligence that he felt as if there were a serpent peeping out of them, and although she had done him so much service only the night before, he was by no means very certain that she would not do him an equally great mischief before sunset. These enchantresses, you must know, are never to be depended upon.

"What says King Æetes, my royal and upright father?" inquired Medea, slightly smiling. "Will he give you the Golden Fleece without any further risk or trouble?"

"On the contrary," answered Jason, "he is very angry with me for taming the brazen bulls and sowing the dragon's teeth. And he forbids me to make any more attempts, and positively refuses to give up the Golden Fleece, whether I slay the dragon or no."

"Yes, Jason," said the princess, "and I can tell you more. Unless you set sail from Colchis before tomorrow's sunrise, the king means to burn your fifty-oared galley and put yourself and your forty-nine brave comrades to the sword. But be of good courage. The Golden Fleece you shall have if it lies within the power of my enchantments to get it for you. Wait for me here an hour before midnight."

At the appointed hour you might again have seen Prince Jason and the Princess Medea, side by side, stealing through the streets of Colchis on their way to the sacred grove, in the center of which the Golden Fleece was suspended to a tree. While they were crossing the pasture ground the brazen bulls came toward Jason, lowing, nodding their heads and thrusting forth their snouts, which, as other cattle do, they loved to have rubbed and caressed by a friendly hand. Their fierce nature was thoroughly tamed; and with their fierceness, the two furnaces in their stomachs had likewise been extinguished, insomuch that they probably enjoyed far more comfort in grazing and chewing their cuds than ever before. Indeed, it had heretofore been a great inconvenience to these poor animals that, whenever they wished to eat a mouthful of grass, the fire out of their nostrils had shriveled it up before they could manage to crop it. How they contrived to keep themselves alive is more than I can imagine. But now, instead of emitting jets of flame and streams of sulphurous vapor, they breathed the very sweetest of cow breath.

After kindly patting the bulls, Jason followed Medea's guidance into the Grove of Mars, where the great oak trees that had been growing for centuries threw so thick a shade that the moonbeams struggled vainly to find their way through it. Only here and there a glimmer fell upon the leaf-strewn earth, or now and then a breeze stirred the boughs aside and gave Jason a glimpse of the sky, lest in that deep obscurity he might forget that there was one overhead. At length, when they had gone further and further into the heart of the duskiness, Medea squeezed Jason's hand.

"Look yonder," she whispered. "Do you see it?"

Gleaming among the venerable oaks there was a radiance, not like the moonbeams, but rather resembling the golden glory of the setting sun. It proceeded from an object which appeared to be suspended at about a man's height from the ground, a little further within the wood.

"What is it?" asked Jason.

"Have you come so far to seek it," exclaimed Medea, "and do you not recognize the meed of all your toils and perils when it glitters before your eyes? It is the Golden Fleece."

Jason went onward a few steps further, and then stopped to gaze. Oh, how beautiful it looked, shining with a marvelous light of its own, that inestimable prize which so many heroes had longed to behold, but had perished in the quest of it, either by the perils of their voyage or by the fiery breath of the brazen-lunged bulls.

"How gloriously it shines!" cried Jason in a rapture. "It has surely been dipped in the richest gold of sunset. Let me hasten onward and take it to my bosom."

"Stay," said Medea, holding him back. "Have you forgotten what guards it?"

To say the truth, in the joy of beholding the object of his desires, the terrible dragon had quite slipped out of Jason's memory. Soon, however, something came to pass that reminded him what perils were still to be encountered. An antelope that probably mistook the yellow radiance for sunrise came bounding fleetly through the grove. He was rushing straight toward the Golden Fleece, when suddenly there was a frightful hiss and the immense head and half the scaly body of the dragon was thrust forth (for he was twisted round the trunk of the tree on which the fleece hung), and seizing the poor antelope, swallowed him with one snap of his jaws.

After this feat, the dragon seemed sensible that some other living creature was within reach, on which he felt inclined to finish his meal. In various directions he kept poking his ugly snout among the trees, stretching out his neck a terrible long way, now here, now there and now close to the spot where Jason and the princess were hiding behind an oak. Upon my word, as the head came waving and undulating through the air and reaching almost within arm's length of Prince Jason, it was a very hideous and uncomfortable sight. The gape of his enormous jaws was nearly as wide as the gateway of the king's palace.

"Well, Jason," whispered Medea (for she was ill natured, as all enchantresses are, and wanted to make the bold youth tremble), "what do you think now of your prospect of winning the Golden Fleece?"

Jason answered only by drawing his sword and making a step forward.

"Stay, foolish youth," said Medea, grasping his arm. "Do not you see you are lost without me as your good angel? In this gold box I have a magic potion which will do the dragon's business far more effectually than your sword."

The dragon had probably heard the voices, for swift as lightning his black head and forked tongue came hissing among the trees again, darting full forty feet at a stretch. As it approached, Medea tossed the contents of the gold box right down the monster's wide-open throat. Immediately, with an outrageous hiss and a tremendous wriggle—flinging his tail up to the tip-top of the tallest tree and shattering all its branches as it crashed heavily down again—the dragon fell at full length upon the ground and lay quite motionless.

"It is only a sleeping potion," said the enchantress to Prince Jason. "One always finds a use for these mischievous creatures sooner or later; so I did not wish to kill him outright. Quick! Snatch the prize and let us begone. You have won the Golden Fleece."

Jason caught the fleece from the tree and hurried through the grove, the deep shadows of which were illuminated as he passed, by the golden glory of the precious object that he bore along. A little way before him he beheld the old woman whom he had helped over the stream, with her peacock beside her. She clapped her hands for joy, and beckoning him to haste, disappeared among the duskiness of the trees. Espying the two winged sons of the North Wind (who were disporting themselves in the moonlight a few hundred feet aloft), Jason bade them tell the rest of the Argonauts to embark as speedily as possible. But Lynceus, with his sharp eyes, had already caught a glimpse of him, bringing the Golden Fleece, although several stone walls, a hill, and the black shadows of the Grove of Mars intervened between. By his advice the heroes had seated themselves on the benches of the galley, with their oars held perpendicularly, ready to let fall into the water.

As Jason drew near he heard the Talking Image calling to him with more than ordinary eagerness, in its grave, sweet voice:

"Make haste, Prince Jason! For your life, make haste!"

With one bound he leaped aboard. At sight of the glorious radiance of the Golden Fleece, the forty-nine heroes gave a mighty shout, and Orpheus, striking his harp, sang a song of triumph, to the cadence of which the galley flew over the water, homeward bound, as if careering along with wings!

The Cyclops

When the great city of Troy was taken, all the chiefs who had fought against it set sail for their homes. But there was wrath in heaven against them, for indeed they had borne themselves haughtily and cruelly in the day of their victory. Therefore they did not all find a safe and happy return. For one was shipwrecked and another was shamefully slain by his false wife in his palace, and others found all things at home troubled and changed and were driven to seek new dwellings elsewhere. And some, whose wives and friends and people had been still true to them through those ten long years of absence, were driven far and wide about the world before they saw their native land again. And of all, the wise Ulysses was he who wandered farthest and suffered most.

He was well-nigh the last to sail, for he had tarried many days to do pleasure to Agamemnon, lord of all the Greeks. Twelve ships he had with him — twelve he had brought to Troy — and in each there were some fifty men, being scarce half of those that had sailed in them in the old days, so many valiant heroes slept the last sleep by Simoïs and Scamander and in the plain and on the seashore, slain in battle or by the shafts of Apollo.

First they sailed northwest to the Thracian coast, where the Ciconians dwelt, who had helped the men of Troy. Their city they took, and in it much plunder, slaves and oxen, and jars of fragrant wine, and might have escaped unhurt, but that they stayed to hold revel on the shore. For the Ciconians gathered their neighbors, being men of the same blood, and did battle with the invaders and drove them to their ship. And when Ulysses numbered his men, he found that he had lost six out of each ship.

Scarce had he set out again when the wind began to blow fiercely; so, seeing a smooth, sandy beach, they drove the ships ashore and dragged them out of reach of the waves, and waited till the storm should abate. And the third morning being fair, they sailed again and journeyed prosperously till they came to the very end of the great Peloponnesian land, where Cape Malea looks out upon the southern sea. But contrary currents baffled them, so that they could not round it, and the north wind blew so strongly that they must fain drive before it. And on the tenth day they came to the land where the lotus grows— a wondrous fruit, of which whosoever eats cares not to see country or wife or children again. Now the Lotus Eaters, for so they call the people of the land, were a kindly folk and gave of the fruit to some of the sailors, not meaning them any harm, but thinking it to be the best that they had to give. These, when they had eaten, said that they would not sail any more over the sea; which, when the wise Ulysses heard, he bade their comrades bind them and carry them, sadly complaining, to the ships.

Then, the wind having abated, they took to their oars and rowed for many days till they came to the country where the Cyclopes dwell. Now, a mile or so from the shore there was an island, very fair and fertile, but no man dwells there or tills the soil, and in the island a harbor where a ship may be safe from all winds, and at the head of the harbor a stream falling from the rock, and whispering alders all about it. Into this the ships passed safely and were hauled up on the beach, and the crews slept by them, waiting for the morning. And the next day they hunted the wild goats, of which there was great store on the island, and feasted right merrily on what they caught, with draughts of red wine which they had carried off from the town of the Ciconians.

But on the morrow, Ulysses, for he was ever fond of adventure and would know of every land to which he came what manner of men they were that dwelt there, took one of his twelve ships and bade row to the land. There was a great hill sloping to the shore, and there rose up here and there a smoke from the caves where the Cyclopes dwelt apart, holding no converse with each other, for they were a rude and savage folk, but ruled each his own household, not caring for others. Now very close to the shore was one of these caves, very huge and deep, with laurels round about the mouth, and in front a fold with walls built of rough stone and shaded by tall oaks and pines. So Ulysses chose out of the crew the twelve bravest, and bade the rest guard the ship, and went to see what manner of dwelling this was and who abode there. He had his sword by his side, and on his shoulder a mighty skin of wine, sweet smelling and strong, with which he might win the heart of some fierce savage, should he chance to meet with such, as indeed his prudent heart forecasted that he might.

So they entered the cave and judged that it was the dwelling of some rich and skilful shepherd. For within there were pens for the young of the sheep and of the goats, divided all according to their age, and there were baskets full of cheeses, and full milk pails ranged along the wall. But the Cyclops himself was away in the pastures. Then the companions of Ulysses besought him that he would depart, taking with him, if he would, a store of cheeses and sundry of the lambs and of the kids. But he would not, for he wished to see, after his wont, what manner of host this strange shepherd might be. And truly he saw it to his cost!

It was evening when the Cyclops came home, a mighty giant, twenty feet in height or more. On his shoulder he bore a vast bundle of pine logs for his fire, and threw them down outside the cave with a great crash, and drove the flocks within, and closed the entrance with a huge rock, which twenty wagons and more could not bear. Then he milked the ewes and all the she-goats, and half of the milk he curdled for cheese and half he set ready for himself when he should sup. Next he kindled a fire with the pine logs, and the flame lighted up all the cave, showing Ulysses and his comrades.

"Who are ye?" cried Polyphemus, for that was the giant's name. "Are ye traders or, haply, pirates?"

For in those days it was not counted shame to be called a pirate.

Ulysses shuddered at the dreadful voice and shape, but bore him bravely, and answered, "We are no pirates, mighty sir, but Greeks, sailing back from Troy, and subjects of the great King Agamemnon, whose fame is spread from one end of heaven to the other. And we are come to beg hospitality of thee in the name of Zeus, who rewards or punishes hosts and guests according as they be faithful the one to the other, or no."

"Nay," said the giant, "it is but idle talk to tell me of Zeus and the other gods. We Cyclopes take no account of gods, holding ourselves to be much better and stronger than they. But come, tell me where have you left your ship?"

But Ulysses saw his thought when he asked about the ship, how he was minded to break it and take from them all hope of flight. Therefore he answered him craftily:

"Ship have we none, for that which was ours King Poseidon brake, driving it on a jutting rock on this coast, and we whom thou seest are all that are escaped from the waves."

Polyphemus answered nothing, but without more ado caught up two of the men, as a man might catch up the whelps of a dog, and dashed them on the ground, and tore them limb from limb and devoured them, with huge draughts of milk between, leaving not a morsel, not even the very bones. But the others, when they saw the dreadful deed, could only weep and pray to Zeus for help. And when the giant had ended his foul meal, he lay down among his sheep and slept.

Then Ulysses questioned much in his heart whether he should slay the monster as he slept, for he doubted not that his good sword would pierce to the giant's heart, mighty as he was.

But, being very wise, he remembered that, should he slay him, he and his comrades would yet perish miserably. For who should move away the great rock that lay against the door of the cave? So they waited till the morning. And the monster woke and milked his flocks, and afterward, seizing two men, devoured them for his meal. Then he went to the pastures, but put the great rock on the mouth of the cave, just as a man puts down the lid upon his quiver.

All that day the wise Ulysses was thinking what he might best do to save himself and his companions, and the end of his thinking was this: There was a mighty pole in the cave, green wood of an olive tree, big as a ship's mast, which Polyphemus purposed to use, when the smoke should have dried it, as a walking staff. Of this he cut off a fathom's length, and his comrades sharpened it and hardened it in the fire and then hid it away. At evening the giant came back and drove his sheep into the cave, nor left the rams outside, as he had been wont to do before, but shut them in. And having duly done his shepherd's work, he made his cruel feast as before. Then Ulysses came forward with the wine skin in his hand and said:

"Drink, Cyclops, now that thou hast feasted. Drink and see what precious things we had in our ship. But no one hereafter will come to thee with such like, if thou dealest with strangers as cruelly as thou hast dealt with us."

Then the Cyclops drank and was mightily pleased, and said, "Give me again to drink and tell me thy name, stranger, and I will give thee a gift such as a host should give. In good truth this is a rare liquor. We, too, have vines, but they bear no wine like this, which indeed must be such as the gods drink in heaven."

Then Ulysses gave him the cup again and he drank. Thrice he gave it to him and thrice he drank, not knowing what it was and how it would work within his brain.

Then Ulysses spake to him. "Thou didst ask my name, Cyclops. Lo! my name is No Man. And now that thou knowest my name, thou shouldst give me thy gift."

And he said, "My gift shall be that I will eat thee last of all thy company."

And as he spake he fell back in a drunken sleep. Then Ulysses bade his comrades be of good courage, for the time was come when they should be delivered. And they thrust the stake of olive wood into the fire till it was ready, green as it was, to burst into flame, and they thrust it into the monster's eye; for he had but one eye, and that in the midst of his forehead, with the eyebrow below it. And Ulysses leaned with all his force upon the stake and thrust it in with might and main. And the burning wood hissed in the eye, just as the red-hot iron hisses in the water when a man seeks to temper steel for a sword.

Then the giant leapt up and tore away the stake and cried aloud, so that all the Cyclopes who dwelt on the mountain side heard him and came about his cave, asking him, "What aileth thee, Polyphemus, that thou makest this uproar in the peaceful night, driving away sleep? Is any one robbing thee of thy sheep or seeking to slay thee by craft or force?"

And the giant answered, "No Man slays me by craft."

"Nay, but," they said, "if no man does thee wrong, we cannot help thee. The sickness which great Zeus may send, who can avoid? Pray to our father, Poseidon, for help."

Then they departed, and Ulysses was glad at heart for the good success of his device when he said that he was No Man.

But the Cyclops rolled away the great stone from the door of the cave and sat in the midst, stretching out his hands to feel whether perchance the men within the cave would seek to go out among the sheep.

Long did Ulysses think how he and his comrades should best escape. At last he lighted upon a good device, and much he thanked Zeus for that this once the giant had driven the rams with the other sheep into the cave. For, these being great and strong, he fastened his comrades under the bellies of the beasts, tying them with osier twigs, of which the giant made his bed. One ram he took and fastened a man beneath it, and two others he set, one on either side. So he did with the six, for but six were left out of the twelve who had ventured with him from the ship.

And there was one mighty ram, far larger than all the others, and to this Ulysses clung, grasping the fleece tight with both his hands. So they waited for the morning. And when the morning came, the rams rushed forth to the pasture; but the giant sat in the door and felt the back of each as it went by, nor thought to try what might be underneath. Last of all went the great ram. And the Cyclops knew him as he passed and said:

"How is this, thou, who art the leader of the flock? Thou art not wont thus to lag behind. Thou hast always been the first to run to the pastures and streams in the morning and the first to come back to the fold when evening fell; and now thou art last of all. Perhaps thou art troubled about thy master's eye, which some wretch—No Man, they call him—has destroyed, having first mastered me with wine. He has not escaped, I ween. I would that thou couldst speak and tell me where he is lurking. Of a truth I would dash out his brains upon the ground and avenge me of this No Man."

So speaking, he let him pass out of the cave. But when they were out of reach of the giant, Ulysses loosed his hold of the ram and then unbound his comrades. And they hastened to their ship, not forgetting to drive before them a good store of the Cyclops' fat sheep. Right glad were those that had abode by the ship to see them. Nor did they lament for those that had died, though they were fain to do so, for Ulysses forbade, fearing lest the noise of their weeping should betray them to the giant, where they were. Then they all climbed into the ship, and sitting well in order on the benches, smote the sea with their oars, laying-to right lustily, that they might the sooner get away from the accursed land. And when they had rowed a hundred yards or so, so that a man's voice could yet be heard by one who stood upon the shore, Ulysses stood up in the ship and shouted:

"He was no coward, O Cyclops, whose comrades thou didst so foully slay in thy den. Justly art thou punished, monster, that devourest thy guests in thy dwelling. May the gods make thee suffer yet worse things than these!"

Then the Cyclops in his wrath broke off the top of a great hill, a mighty rock, and hurled it where he had heard the voice.

Right in front of the ship's bow it fell, and a great wave rose as it sank, and washed the ship back to the shore. But Ulysses seized a long pole with both hands and pushed the ship from the land and bade his comrades ply their oars, nodding with his head, for he was too wise to speak, lest the Cyclops should know where they were. Then they rowed with all their might and main.

And when they had gotten twice as far as before, Ulysses made as if he would speak again; but his comrades sought to hinder him, saying, "Nay, my lord, anger not the giant any more. Surely we thought before we were lost, when he threw the great rock and washed our ship back to the shore. And if he hear thee now, he may crush our ship and us, for the man throws a mighty bolt and throws it far."

But Ulysses would not be persuaded, but stood up and said, "Hear, Cyclops! If any man ask who blinded thee, say that it was the warrior Ulysses, son of Laertes, dwelling in Ithaca."

And the Cyclops answered with a groan, "Of a truth, the old oracles are fulfilled, for long ago there came to this land one Telemus, a prophet, and dwelt among us even to old age. This man foretold me that one Ulysses would rob me of my sight. But I looked for a great man and a strong, who should subdue me by force, and now a weakling has done the deed, having cheated me with wine. But come thou hither, Ulysses, and I will be a host indeed to thee. Or, at least, may Poseidon give thee such a voyage to thy home as I would wish thee to have. For know that Poseidon is my sire. May be that he may heal me of my grievous wound."

And Ulysses said, "Would to God, I could send thee down to the abode of the dead, where thou wouldst be past all healing, even from Poseidon's self."

Then Cyclops lifted up his hands to Poseidon and prayed:

"Hear me, Poseidon, if I am indeed thy son and thou my father. May this Ulysses never reach his home! or, if the Fates have ordered that he should reach it, may he come alone, all his comrades lost, and come to find sore trouble in his house!"

And as he ended he hurled another mighty rock, which almost lighted on the rudder's end, yet missed it as if by a hair's breadth. So Ulysses and his comrades escaped and came to the island of the wild goats, where they found their comrades, who indeed had waited long for them, in sore fear lest they had perished. Then Ulysses divided among his company all the sheep which they had taken from the Cyclops. And all, with one consent, gave him for his share the great ram which had carried him out of the cave, and he sacrificed it to Zeus. And all that day they feasted right merrily on the flesh of sheep and on sweet wine, and when the night was come, they lay down upon the shore and slept.

Œdipus And The Sphinx

It befell in times past that the gods, being angry with the inhabitants of Thebes, sent into their land a very troublesome beast which men called the Sphinx. Now this beast had the face and breast of a fair woman, but the feet and claws of a lion; and it was wont to ask a riddle of such as encountered it, and such as answered not aright it would tear and devour.

When it had laid waste the land many days, there chanced to come to Thebes one Œdipus, who had fled from the city of Corinth that he might escape the doom which the gods had spoken against him. And the men of the place told him of the Sphinx, how she cruelly devoured the people, and that he who should deliver them from her should have the kingdom. So Œdipus, being very bold, and also ready of wit, went forth to meet the monster. And when she saw him she spake, saying:

"Read me this riddle right, or die:
What liveth there beneath the sky,
Four-footed creature that doth choose
Now three feet and now twain to use,
And still more feebly o'er the plain
Walketh with three feet than with twain?"

And Œdipus made reply:

"'Tis man, who in life's early day
Four-footed crawleth on his way;
When time hath made his strength complete,
Upright his form and twain his feet;
When age hath bound him to the ground
A third foot in his staff is found."

And when the Sphinx found that her riddle was answered she cast herself from a high rock and perished.

As a reward Œdipus received the great kingdom of Thebes and the hand of the widowed queen Jocasta in marriage. Four children were born to them—two sons, Eteocles and Polynices, and two daughters, Antigone and Ismené.

Now the gods had decreed that Œdipus should murder his own father and marry his own mother, and by a curious chance this was precisely what he had done. As a baby he had been left to die lest he should live to fulfil the doom, but had been rescued by an old shepherd and brought up at the court of Corinth. Fleeing from there that he might not murder him whom he believed to be his father, he had come to Thebes, and on the way had met Laius, his true father, the king, and killed him.

While he remained ignorant of the facts Œdipus was very happy and reigned in great power and glory; but when pestilence fell upon the land and he discovered the truth of the almost forgotten oracle, he was very miserable, and in the madness of grief put out his own eyes.

Antigone, A Faithful Daughter And Sister

Jocasta, when she learned that Œdipus was really her son, was so filled with horror and distress that she took her own life. But Antigone and Ismené were sorry for their father, whom they loved very dearly, and sought by every means they knew to render his suffering less.

Longing to see again the land of Corinth which he had left seized the blind Œdipus, and like a beggar, staff in hand, he set out. Only Antigone accompanied him, guiding his step and striving daily to keep up his courage.

After much wandering Œdipus was finally cast into prison. Then the two sons took possession of the kingdom, making agreement between themselves that each should reign for the space of one year. And the elder of the two, whose name was Eteocles, first had the kingdom; but when his year was come to an end, he would not abide by his promise, but kept that which he should have given up, and drove out his younger brother from the city. Then the younger, whose name was Polynices, fled to Argos, to King Adrastus. And after a while he married the daughter of the king, who made a covenant with him that he would bring him back with a high hand to Thebes and set him on the throne of his father. Then the king sent messengers to certain of the princes of Greece, entreating that they would help in this matter. And of these some would not, but others hearkened to his words, so that a great army was gathered together and followed the king and Polynices to make war against Thebes. So they came and pitched their camp over against the city. And after they had been there many days, the battle grew fierce about the wall. But the chiefest fight was between the two brothers, for the two came together in an open space before the gates. And first Polynices prayed to Heré, for she was the goddess of the great city of Argos, which had helped him in this enterprise, and Eteocles prayed to Pallas of the Golden Shield, whose temple stood hard by. Then they crouched, each covered with his shield and holding his spear in his hand, if by chance his enemy should give occasion to smite him; and if one showed so much as an eye above the rim of his shield the other would strike at him. But after a while King Eteocles slipped upon a stone that was under his foot, and uncovered his leg, at which straightway Polynices took aim with his spear, piercing the skin. But so doing he laid his own shoulder bare, and King Eteocles gave him a wound in the breast. He brake his spear in striking and would have fared ill but that with a great stone he smote the spear of Polynices and brake this also in the middle. And now were the two equal, for each had lost his spear. So they drew their swords and came yet closer together. But Eteocles used a device which he had learnt in the land of Thessaly; for he drew his left foot back, as if he would have ceased from the battle, and then of a sudden moved the right forward; and so smiting sideways, drove his sword right through the body of Polynices. But when, thinking that he had slain him, he set his weapons in the earth and began to spoil him of his arms, the other, for he yet breathed a little, laid his hand upon his sword, and though he had scarce strength to smite, yet gave the king a mortal blow, so that the two lay dead together on the plain. And the men of Thebes lifted up the bodies of the dead and bare them both into the city.

When these two brothers, the sons of King Œdipus, had fallen each by the hand of the other, the kingdom fell to Creon, their uncle. For not only was he the next of kin to the dead, but also the people held him in great honor because his son Menœceus had offered himself with a willing heart that he might deliver his city from captivity.

Now when Creon was come to the throne he made a proclamation about the two princes, commanding that they should bury Eteocles with all honor, seeing that he died as beseemed a good man and a brave, doing battle for his country, that it should not be delivered into the hands of the enemy; but as for Polynices, he bade them leave his body to be devoured by the fowls of the air and the beasts of the field, because he had joined himself to the enemy and would have beaten down the walls of the city and burned the temples of the gods with fire and led the people captive. Also he commanded that if any man should break this decree he should suffer death by stoning.

Now Antigone, who was sister to the two princes, heard that the decree had gone forth, and chancing to meet her sister Ismené before the gates of the palace, spake to her, saying:

"O my sister, hast thou heard this decree that the king hath put forth concerning our brethren that are dead?"

Then Ismené made answer: "I have heard nothing, my sister, only that we are bereaved of both of our brethren in one day and that the army of the Argives is departed in this night that is now past. So much I know, but no more."

"Hearken then. King Creon hath made a proclamation that they shall bury Eteocles with all honor, but that Polynices shall lie unburied, that the birds of the air and the beasts of the field may devour him, and that whosoever shall break this decree shall suffer death by stoning."

"But if it be so, my sister, how can we avail to change it?"

"Think whether or no thou wilt share with me the doing of this deed."

"What deed? What meanest thou?"

"To pay due honor to this dead body."

"What? Wilt thou bury him when the king hath forbidden it?"

"Yes, for he is my brother and also thine, though perchance thou wouldst not have it so. And I will not play him false."

"O my sister, wilt thou do this when Creon hath forbidden it?"

"Why should he stand between me and mine?"

"But think now what sorrows are come upon our house. For our father perished miserably, having first put out his own eyes; and our mother hanged herself with her own hands; our two brothers fell in one day, each by the other's spear; and now we two only are left. And shall we not fall into a worse destruction than any, if we transgress these commands of the king? Think, too, that we are women and not men, and of necessity obey them that are stronger. Wherefore, as for me, I will pray the dead to pardon me, seeing that I am thus constrained; but I will obey them that rule."

"I advise thee not, and if thou thinkest thus, I would not have thee for helper. But know that I will bury my brother, nor could I better die than for doing such a deed. For as he loved me, so also do I love him greatly. And shall not I do pleasure to the dead rather than to the living, seeing that I shall abide with the dead for ever? But thou, if thou wilt do dishonor to the laws of the gods?"

"I dishonor them not. Only I cannot set myself against the powers that be."

"So be it; but I will bury my brother."

"O my sister, how I fear for thee!"

"Fear for thyself. Thine own lot needeth all thy care."

"Thou wilt at least keep thy counsel, nor tell the thing to any man."

"Not so: hide it not. I shall scorn thee more if thou proclaim it not aloud to all."

So Antigone departed; and after a while came to the same place King Creon, clad in his royal robes and with his scepter in his hand, and set forth his counsel to the elders who were assembled, how he had dealt with the two princes according to their deserving, giving all honor to him that loved his country and casting forth the other unburied. And he bade them take care that this decree should be kept, saying that he had also appointed certain men to watch the dead body.

And he had scarcely left speaking when there came one of these same watchers and said:

"I have not come hither in haste, O King; nay, I doubted much, while I was yet on the way, whether I should not turn again. For now I thought, 'Fool, why goest thou where thou shalt suffer for it'; and then, again, 'Fool, the king will hear the matter elsewhere, and then how wilt thou fare?' But at the last I came as I had purposed, for I know that nothing may happen to me contrary to fate."

"But say," said the king, "what troubles thee so much?"

"First hear my case. I did not the thing and know not who did it, and it were a grievous wrong should I fall into trouble for such a cause."

"Thou makest a long preface, excusing thyself, but yet hast, as I judge, something to tell."

"Fear, my lord, ever causeth delay."

"Wilt thou not speak out thy news and then begone?"

"I will speak it. Know then that some man hath thrown dust upon this dead corpse, and done besides such things as are needful."

"What sayest thou? Who hath dared to do this deed?"

"That I know not, for there was no mark as of spade or pick-axe; nor was the earth broken, nor had wagon passed thereon. We were sore dismayed when the watchman showed the thing to us; for the body we could not see. Buried indeed it was not, but rather covered with dust. Nor was there any sign as of wild beast or of dog that had torn it. Then there arose a contention among us, each blaming the other, and accusing his fellows, and himself denying that he had done the deed or was privy to it. And doubtless we had fallen to blows but that one spake a word which made us all tremble for fear, knowing that it must be as he said. For he said that the thing must be told to thee, and in no wise hidden. So we drew lots, and by evil chance the lot fell upon me. Wherefore I am here, not willingly, for no man loveth him that bringeth evil tidings."

Then said the chief of the old men:

"Consider, O King, for haply this thing is from the gods."

But the king cried:

"Thinkest thou that the gods care for such an one as this dead man, who would have burnt their temples with fire, and laid waste the land which they love, and set at naught the laws? Not so. But there are men in this city who have long time had ill will to me, not bowing their necks to my yoke; and they have persuaded these fellows with money to do this thing. Surely there never was so evil a thing as money, which maketh cities into ruinous heaps and banisheth men from their houses and turneth their thoughts from good unto evil. But as for them that have done this deed for hire, of a truth they shall not escape, for I say to thee, fellow, if ye bring not here before my eyes the man that did this thing, I will hang you up alive. So shall ye learn that ill gains bring no profit to a man."

So the guard departed, but as he went he said to himself:

"Now may the gods grant that the man be found; but however this may be, thou shalt not see me come again on such errand as this, for even now have I escaped beyond all hope."

Notwithstanding, after a space he came back with one of his fellows; and they brought with them the maiden Antigone, with her hands bound together.

And it chanced that at the same time King Creon came forth from the palace. Then the guard set forth the thing to him, saying:

"We cleared away the dust from the dead body, and sat watching it. And when it was now noon, and the sun was at his height, there came a whirlwind over the plain, driving a great cloud of dust. And when this had passed, we looked, and lo! this maiden whom we have brought hither stood by the dead corpse. And when she saw that it lay bare as before, she sent up an exceeding bitter cry, even as a bird whose young ones have been taken from the nest. Then she cursed them that had done this deed, and brought dust and sprinkled it upon the dead man, and poured water upon him three times. Then we ran and laid hold upon her and accused her that she had done this deed;

and she denied it not. But as for me, 'tis well to have escaped from death, but it is ill to bring friends into the same. Yet I hold that there is nothing dearer to a man than his life."

Then said the king to Antigone:

"Tell me in a word, didst thou know my decree?"

"I knew it. Was it not plainly declared?"

"How daredst thou to transgress the laws?"

"Zeus made not such laws, nor Justice that dwelleth with the gods below. I judged not that thy decrees had such authority that a man should transgress for them the unwritten sure commandments of the gods. For these, indeed, are not of today or yesterday, but they live forever, and their beginning no man knoweth. Should I, for fear of thee, be found guilty against them? That I should die I knew. Why not? All men must die. And if I die before my time, what loss? He who liveth among many sorrows even as I have lived, counteth it gain to die. But had I left my own mother's son unburied, this had been loss indeed."

Then said the king:

"Such stubborn thoughts have a speedy fall and are shivered even as the iron that hath been made hard in the furnace. And as for this woman and her sister—for I judge her sister to have had a part in this matter—though they were nearer to me than all my kindred, yet shall they not escape the doom of death. Wherefore let some one bring the other woman hither."

And while they went to fetch the maiden Ismené, Antigone said to the king:

"Is it not enough for thee to slay me? What need to say more? For thy words please me not, nor mine thee. Yet what nobler thing could I have done than to bury my mother's son? And so would all men say, but fear shutteth their mouths."

"Nay," said the king, "none of the children of Cadmus thinketh thus, but thou only. But, hold, was not he that fell in battle with this man thy brother also?"

"Yes, truly, my brother he was."

"And dost thou not dishonor him when thou honorest his enemy?"

"The dead man would not say it, could he speak."

"Shall then the wicked have like honor with the good?"

"How knowest thou but that such honor pleaseth the gods below?"

"I have no love for them I hate, though they be dead."

"Of hating I know nothing; 'tis enough for me to love."

"If thou wilt love, go love the dead. But while I live no woman shall rule me."

Then those that had been sent to fetch the maiden Ismené brought her forth from the palace. And when the king accused her that she had been privy to the deed she denied not, but would have shared one lot with her sister.

But Antigone turned from her, saying:

"Not so; thou hast no part or lot in the matter. For thou hast chosen life and I have chosen death; and even so shall it be."

And when Ismené saw that she prevailed nothing with her sister, she turned to the king and said:

"Wilt thou slay the bride of thy son?"

"Ay," said he, "there are other brides to win!"

"But none," she made reply, "that accord so well with him."

"I will have no evil wives for my sons," said the king.

Then cried Antigone:

"O Hæmon, whom I love, how thy father wrongeth thee!"

Then the king bade the guards lead the two into the palace. But scarcely had they gone when there came to the place the Prince Hæmon, the king's son, who was betrothed to the maiden Antigone. And when the king saw him, he said:

"Art thou content, my son, with thy father's judgment?"

And the young man answered:

"My father, I would follow thy counsels in all things."

Then said the king:

"'Tis well spoken, my son. This is a thing to be desired, that a man should have obedient children. But if it be otherwise with a man, he hath gotten great trouble for himself and maketh sport for them that hate him. And now as to this matter. There is naught worse than an evil wife. Wherefore I say let this damsel wed a bridegroom among the dead. For since I have found her, alone of all this people, breaking my decree, surely she shall die. Nor shall it profit her to claim kinship with me, for he that would rule a city must first deal justly with his own kindred. And as for obedience, this it is that maketh a city to stand both in peace and in war."

To this the Prince Hæmon made answer:

"What thou sayest, my father, I do not judge. Yet bethink thee, that I see and hear on thy behalf what is hidden from thee. For common men cannot abide thy look if they say that which pleaseth thee not. Yet do I hear it in secret. Know then that all the city mourneth for this maiden, saying that she dieth wrongfully for a very noble deed, in that she buried her brother. And 'tis well, my father, not to be wholly set on thy thoughts, but to listen to the counsels of others."

"Nay," said the king; "shall I be taught by such an one as thou?"

"I pray thee regard my words, if they be well, and not my years."

"Can it be well to honor them that transgress? And hath not this woman transgressed?"

"The people of this city judge not so."

"The people, sayest thou? Is it for them to rule, or for me?"

"No city is the possession of one man only."

So the two answered one the other, and their anger waxed hot. And at the last the king cried:

"Bring this accursed woman and slay her before his eyes."

And the prince answered:

"That thou shalt never do. And know this also, that thou shalt never see my face again."

So he went away in a rage; and the old men would have appeased the king's wrath, but he would not hearken to them, but said that the two maidens should die.

"Wilt thou then slay them both?" said the old men.

"'Tis well said," the king made answer. "Her that meddled not with the matter, I harm not."

"And how wilt thou deal with the other?"

"There is a desolate place, and there I will shut her up alive in a sepulchre; yet giving her so much of food as shall quit us of guilt in the matter, for I would not have the city defiled. There let her persuade Death, whom she loveth so much, that he harm her not."

So the guards led Antigone away to shut her up alive in the sepulchre. But scarcely had they departed when there came an old prophet Tiresias, seeking the king. Blind he was, so that a boy led him by the hand; but the gods had given him to see things to come.

And when the king saw him he asked:

"What seekest thou, wisest of men?"

Then the prophet answered:

"Hearken, O King, and I will tell thee. I sat in my seat, after my custom, in the place whither all manner of birds resort. And as I sat I heard a cry of birds that I knew not, very strange and full of wrath. And I knew that they tare and slew each other, for I heard the fierce flapping of their wings. And being afraid, I made inquiry about the fire, how it burned upon the altars. And this boy, for as I am a guide to others so he guideth me, told me that it shone not at all, but smouldered and was dull, and that the flesh which was burnt upon the altar spluttered in the flame and wasted away into corruption and filthiness. And now I tell thee, O King, that the city is troubled by thy ill counsels. For the dogs and the birds of the air tear the flesh of this dead son of Œdipus, whom thou sufferest not to have due burial, and carry it to the altars, polluting them therewith. Wherefore the gods receive not from us prayer or sacrifice, and the cry of the birds hath an evil sound, for they are full of the flesh of a man. Therefore I bid thee be wise in time. For all men may err; but he that keepeth not his folly, but repenteth, doeth well; but stubbornness cometh to great trouble."

Then the king answered:

"Old man, I know the race of prophets full well, how ye sell your art for gold. But make thy trade as thou wilt, this man shall not have burial; yea, though the eagles of Zeus carry his flesh to their master's throne in heaven, he shall not have it."

And when the prophet spake again, entreating him and warning, the king answered him after the same fashion, that he spake not honestly, but had sold his art for money.

But at the last the prophet spake in great wrath, saying:

"Know, O King, that before many days shall pass thou shalt pay a life for a life, even one of thine own children, for them with whom thou hast dealt unrighteously, shutting up the living with the dead and keeping the dead from them to whom they belong. Therefore the Furies lie in wait for thee and thou shalt see whether or no I speak these things for money. For there shall be mourning and lamentation in thine own house, and against thy people shall be stirred up many cities. And now, my child, lead me home and let this man rage against them that are younger than I."

So the prophet departed and the old men were sore afraid and said:

"He hath spoken terrible things, O King; nor ever since these gray hairs were black have we known him say that which was false."

"Even so," said the king, "and I am troubled in heart and yet am loath to depart from my purpose."

"King Creon," said the old men, "thou needest good counsel."

"What, then, would ye have done?"

"Set free the maiden from the sepulchre and give this dead man burial."

Then the king cried to his people that they should bring bars wherewith to loosen the doors of the sepulchre, and hastened with them to the place. But coming on their way to the body of Prince Polynices, they took it up and washed it, and buried that which remained of it, and raised over the ashes a great mound of earth. And this being done, they drew near to the place of the sepulchre; and as they approached, the king heard within a very piteous voice, and knew it for the voice of his son. Then he bade his attendants loose the door with all speed; and when they had loosed it, they beheld within a very piteous sight. For the maiden Antigone had hanged herself by the girdle of linen which she wore, and the young man Prince Hæmon stood with his arms about her dead body, embracing it. And when the king saw him, he cried to him to come forth; but the prince glared fiercely upon him and answered him not a word, but drew his two-edged sword. Then the king, thinking that his son was minded in his madness to slay him, leapt back, but the prince drove the sword into his own heart and fell forward on the earth, still holding the dead maiden in his arms. And when they brought the tidings of these things to Queen Eurydice, the wife of King Creon and mother to the prince, she could not endure the grief, being thus bereaved of her children, but laid hold of a sword and slew herself therewith.

So the house of King Creon was left desolate unto him that day, because he despised the ordinances of the gods.

The Story Of Iphigenia

King Agamemnon sat in his tent at Aulis, where the army of the Greeks was gathered together, being about to sail against the great city of Troy. And it was now past midnight; but the king slept not, for he was careful and troubled about many things. And he had a lamp before him and in his hand a tablet of pine wood, whereon he wrote. But he seemed not to remain in the same mind about that which he wrote; for now he would blot out the letters, and then would write them again; and now he fastened the seal upon the tablet and then brake it. And as he did this he wept and was like to a man distracted. But after a while he called to an old man, his attendant (the man had been given in time past by Tyndareus to his daughter, Queen Clytæmnestra) and said:

"Old man, thou knowest how Calchas the soothsayer bade me offer for a sacrifice to Artemis, who is goddess of this place, my daughter Iphigenia, saying that so only should the army have a prosperous voyage from this place to Troy, and should take the city and destroy it; and how when I heard these words I bade Talthybius the herald go throughout the army and bid them depart, every man to his own country, for that I would not do this thing; and how my brother, King Menelaüs, persuaded me so that I consented to it. Now, therefore, hearken to this, for what I am about to tell thee three men only know, namely, Calchas the soothsayer, and Menelaüs, and Ulysses, king of Ithaca. I wrote a letter to my wife the queen, that she should send her daughter to this place, that she might be married to King Achilles; and I magnified the man to her, saying that he would in no wise sail with us unless I would give him my daughter in marriage. But now I have changed my purpose and have written another letter after this fashion, as I will now set forth to thee: 'Daughter of Leda, send not thy child to the land of Eubœa, for I will give her in marriage at another time.'"

"Aye," said the old man, "but how wilt thou deal with King Achilles? Will he not be wroth, hearing that he hath been cheated of his wife?"

"Not so," answered the king, "for we have indeed used his name, but he knoweth nothing of this marriage. And now make haste. Sit not thou down by any fountain in the woods, and suffer not thine eyes to sleep. And beware lest the chariot bearing the queen and her daughter pass thee where the roads divide. And see that thou keep the seal upon this letter unbroken."

So the old man departed with the letter. But scarcely had he left the tent when King Menelaüs spied him and laid hands on him, taking the letter and breaking the seal. And the old man cried out:

"Help, my lord; here is one hath taken thy letter!"

Then King Agamemnon came forth from his tent, saying, "What meaneth this uproar and disputing that I hear?"

And Menelaüs answered, "Seest thou this letter that I hold in my hand?"

"I see it: it is mine. Give it to me."

"I give it not till I have read that which is written therein to all the army of the Greeks."

"Where didst thou find it?"

"I found it while I waited for thy daughter till she should come to the camp."

"What hast thou to do with that? May I not rule my own household?"

Then Menelaüs reproached his brother because he did not continue in one mind. "For first," he said, "before thou wast chosen captain of the host, thou wast all things to all men, greeting every man courteously, and taking him by the hand, and talking with him, and leaving thy doors open to any that would enter; but afterwards, being now chosen, thou wast haughty and hard of access. And next, when this trouble came upon the army, and thou wast sore afraid lest thou shouldst lose thy office and so miss renown, didst thou not hearken to Calchas the soothsayer, and promise thy daughter for sacrifice, and send for her to the camp, making pretence of giving her in marriage to Achilles? And now thou art gone back from thy word. Surely this is an evil day for Greece, that is troubled because thou wantest wisdom."

Then answered King Agamemnon: "What is thy quarrel with me? Why blamest thou me if thou couldst not rule thy wife? And now to win back this woman, because forsooth she is fair, thou castest aside both reason and honor. And I, if I had an ill purpose and now have changed it for that which is wiser, dost thou charge me with folly? Let them that sware the oath to Tyndareus go with thee on this errand. Why should I slay my child and work for myself sorrow and remorse without end that thou mayest have vengeance for thy wicked wife?"

Then Menelaüs turned away in a rage, crying, "Betray me if thou wilt. I will betake myself to other counsels and other friends."

But even as he spake there came a messenger, saying, "King Agamemnon, I am come, as thou badest me, with thy daughter Iphigenia. Also her mother, Queen Clytæmnestra, is come, bringing with her her little son Orestes. And now they are resting themselves and their horses by the side of a spring, for indeed the way is long and weary. And all the army is gathered about them to see them and greet them. And men question much wherefore they are come, saying, 'Doth the king make a marriage for his daughter; or hath he sent for her, desiring to see her?' But I know thy purpose, my lord; wherefore we will dance and shout and make merry, for this is a happy day for the maiden."

But the King Agamemnon was sore dismayed when he knew that the queen was come, and spake to himself, "Now what shall I say to my wife? For that she is rightly come to the marriage of her daughter, who can deny? But what will she say when she knoweth my purpose? And of the maiden, what shall I say? Unhappy maiden whose bridegroom shall be death! For she will cry to me, 'Wilt thou kill me, my father?' And the little Orestes will wail, not knowing what he doeth, seeing he is but a babe. Cursed be Paris, who hath wrought this woe!"

And now King Menelaüs came back, saying that it repented him of what he had said, "For why should thy child die for me? What hath she to do with Helen? Let the army be scattered, so that this wrong be not done."

Then said King Agamemnon, "But how shall I escape from this strait? For the whole host will compel me to this deed?"

"Not so," said King Menelaüs, "if thou wilt send back the maiden to Argos."

"But what shall that profit," said the king; "for Calchas will cause the matter to be known, or Ulysses, saying that I have failed of my promise; and if I fly to Argos, they will come and destroy my city and lay waste my land. Woe is me! in what a strait am I set! But take thou care, my brother, that Clytæmnestra hear nothing of these things."

And when he had ended speaking, the queen herself came unto the tent, riding in a chariot, having her daughter by her side. And she bade one of the attendants take out with care the caskets which she had brought for her daughter, and bade others help her daughter to alight and herself also, and to a fourth she said that he should take the young Orestes. Then Iphigenia greeted her father, saying, "Thou hast done well to send for me, my father."

"'Tis true and yet not true, my child."

"Thou lookest not well pleased to see me, my father."

"He that is a king and commandeth a host hath many cares."

"Put away thy cares awhile and give thyself to me."

"I am glad beyond measure to see thee."

"Glad art thou? Then why dost thou weep?"

"I weep because thou must be long time absent from me."

"Perish all these fightings and troubles!"

"They will cause many to perish, and me most miserably of all."

"Art thou going a journey from me, my father?"

"Aye, and thou also hast a journey to make."

"Must I make it alone, or with my mother?"

"Alone; neither father nor mother may be with thee."

"Sendest thou me to dwell elsewhere?"

"Hold thy peace: such things are not for maidens to inquire."

"Well, my father, order matters with the Phrygians and then make haste to return."

"I must first make a sacrifice to the gods."

"'Tis well. The gods should have due honor."

"Aye, and thou wilt stand close to the altar."

"Shall I lead the dances, my father?"

"O my child, how I envy thee, that thou knowest naught! And now go into the tent; but first kiss me and give me thy hand, for thou shalt be parted from thy father for many days."

And when she was gone within, he cried, "O fair bosom and very lovely cheeks and yellow hair of my child! O city of Priam, what woe thou bringest on me! But I must say no more."

Then he turned to the queen and excused himself that he wept when he should rather have rejoiced for the marriage of his daughter. And when the queen would know of the estate of the bridegroom he told her that his name was Achilles and that he was the son of Peleus by his wife Thetis, the daughter of Nereus of the sea, and that he dwelt in Phthia. And when she inquired of the time of the marriage, he said that it should be in the same moon, on the first lucky day; and as to the place, that it must be where the bridegroom was sojourning, that is to say, in the camp. "And I," said the king, "will give the maiden to her husband."

"But where," answered the queen, "is it your pleasure that I should be?"

"Thou must return to Argos and care for the maidens there."

"Sayest thou that I must return? Who then will hold up the torch for the bride?"

"I will do that which is needful. For it is not seemly that thou shouldst be present where the whole army is gathered together."

"Aye, but it is seemly that a mother should give her daughter in marriage."

"But the maidens at home should not be left alone."

"They are well kept in their chambers."

"Be persuaded, lady."

"Not so: thou shalt order that which is without the house, but I that which is within."

But now came Achilles to tell the king that the army was growing impatient, saying that unless they might sail speedily to Troy they would return each man to his home. And when the queen heard his name—for he had said to the attendant, "Tell thy master that Achilles, the son of Peleus, would speak with him"—she came forth from the tent and greeted him and bade him give her his right hand. And when the young man was ashamed (for it was not counted a seemly thing that men should speak with women) she said:

"But why art thou ashamed, seeing that thou art about to marry my daughter?"

And he answered, "What sayest thou, lady? I cannot speak for wonder at thy words."

"Often men are ashamed when they see new friends and the talk is of marriage."

"But, lady, I never was suitor for thy daughter. Nor have the sons of Atreus said aught to me of the matter."

But the queen was beyond measure astonished, and cried, "Now this is shameful indeed, that I should seek a bridegroom for my daughter in such fashion."

But when Achilles would have departed, to inquire of the king what this thing might mean, the old man that had at the first carried the letter came forth and bade him stay. And when he had assurance that he should receive no harm for what he should tell them, he unfolded the whole matter. And when the queen had heard it, she cried to Achilles, "O son of Thetis of the sea! help me now in this strait and help this maiden that hath been called thy bride, though this indeed be false. 'Twill be a shame to thee if such wrong be done under thy name; for it is thy name that hath undone us. Nor have I any altar to which I may flee, nor any friend but thee only in this army."

Then Achilles made answer, "Lady, I learnt from Chiron, who was the most righteous of men, to be true and honest. And if the sons of Atreus govern according to right, I obey them; and if not, not. Know, then, that thy daughter, seeing that she hath been given, though but in word only, to me, shall not be slain by her father. For if she so die, then shall my name be brought to great dishonor, seeing that through it thou hast been persuaded to come with her to this place. This sword shall see right soon whether any one will dare to take this maiden from me."

And now King Agamemnon came forth, saying that all things were ready for the marriage, and that they waited for the maiden, not knowing that the whole matter had been revealed to the queen. Then she said:

"Tell me now, dost thou purpose to slay thy daughter and mine?" And when he was silent, not knowing, indeed, what to say, she reproached him with many words, that she had been a loving and faithful wife to him, for which he made her an ill recompense slaying her child.

And when she had made an end of speaking, the maiden came forth from the tent, holding the young child Orestes in her arms, and cast herself upon her knees before her father and besought him, saying, "I would, my father, that I had the voice of Orpheus, who made even the rocks to follow him, that I might persuade thee; but now all that I have I give, even these tears. O my father, I am thy child; slay me not before my time. This light is sweet to look upon. Drive me not from it to the land of darkness. I was the first to call thee father; and the first to whom thou didst say 'my child.' And thou wouldst say to me,

'Some day, my child, I shall see thee a happy wife in the home of a good husband.' And I would answer, 'And I will receive thee with all love when thou art old, and pay thee back for all the benefits thou hast done unto me.' This I indeed remember, but thou forgettest; for thou art ready to slay me. Do it not, I beseech thee, by Pelops thy grandsire, and Atreus thy father, and this my mother, who travailed in childbirth of me and now travaileth again in her sorrow. And thou, O my brother, though thou art but a babe, help me. Weep with me; beseech thy father that he slay not thy sister. O my father, though he be silent, yet, indeed, he beseecheth thee. For his sake, therefore, yea, and for mine own, have pity upon me and slay me not."

But the king was sore distracted, knowing not what he should say or do, for a terrible necessity was upon him, seeing that the army could not make their journey to Troy unless this deed should first be done. And while he doubted came Achilles, saying that there was a horrible tumult in the camp, the men crying out that the maiden must be sacrificed, and that when he would have stayed them from their purpose, the people had stoned him with stones, and that his own Myrmidons helped him not, but rather were the first to assail him. Nevertheless, he said that he would fight for the maiden, even to the utmost, and that there were faithful men who would stand with him and help him. But when the maiden heard these words, she stood forth and said, "Hearken to me, my mother. Be not wroth with my father, for we cannot fight against fate. Also we must take thought that this young man suffer not, for his help will avail naught and he himself will perish. Therefore I am resolved to die; for all Greece looketh to me; for without me the ships cannot make their voyage, nor the city of Troy be taken. Thou didst bear me, my mother, not for thyself only, but for this whole people. Wherefore I will give myself for them. Offer me for an offering, and let the Greeks take the city of Troy, for this shall be my memorial forever."

Then said Achilles, "Lady, I should count myself most happy if the gods would grant thee to be my wife. For I love thee well when I see how noble thou art. And if thou wilt, I will carry thee to my home. And I doubt not that I shall save thee, though all the men of Greece be against me."

But the maiden answered, "What I say, I say with full purpose. Nor will I that any man should die for me, but rather will I save this land of Greece."

And Achilles said, "If this be thy will, lady, I cannot say nay, for it is a noble thing that thou doest."

Nor was the maiden turned from her purpose though her mother besought her with many tears. So they that were appointed led her to the grove of Artemis, where there was built an altar, and the whole army of the Greeks gathered about it. But when the king saw her going to her death he covered his face with his mantle; but she stood by him, and said, "I give my body with a willing heart to die for my country and for the whole land of Greece. I pray the gods that ye may prosper and win the victory in this war and come back safe to your homes. And now let no man touch me, for I will die with a good heart."

And all men marveled to see the maiden of what a good courage she was. And all the army stood regarding the maiden and the priest and the altar.

Then there befell a marvelous thing. For suddenly the maiden was not there. Whither she had gone no one knew; but in her stead there lay gasping a great hind, and all the altar was red with the blood thereof.

And Calchas said, "See ye this, men of Greece, how the goddess hath provided this offering in the place of the maiden, for she would not that her altar should be defiled with innocent blood. Be of good courage, therefore, and depart every man to his ship, for this day ye shall sail across the sea to the land of Troy."

Then the goddess carried away the maiden to the land of the Taurians, where she had a temple and an altar. Now on this altar the king of the land was wont to sacrifice any stranger, being Greek by nation, who was driven by stress of weather to the place, for none went thither willingly. And the name of the king was Thoas, which signifieth in the Greek tongue, "swift of foot."

Now when the maiden had been there many years she dreamed a dream. And in the dream she seemed to have departed from the land of the Taurians and to dwell in the city of Argos, wherein she had been born. And as she slept in the women's chamber there befell a great earthquake, and cast to the ground the palace of her fathers, so that there was left one pillar only which stood upright. And as she looked on this pillar, yellow hair seemed to grow upon it as the hair of a man, and it spake with a man's voice. And she did to it as she was wont to do to the strangers that were sacrificed upon the altar, purifying it with water and weeping the while. And the interpretation of the dream she judged to be that her brother Orestes was dead, for that male children are the pillars of a house, and that she only was left to the house of her father.

Now it chanced that at this same time Orestes, with Pylades that was his friend, came in a ship to the land of the Taurians. And the cause of his coming was this. After that he had slain his mother, taking vengeance for the death of King Agamemnon his father, the Furies pursued him. Then Apollo, who had commanded him to do this deed, bade him go to the land of Athens that he might be judged. And when he had been judged and loosed, yet the Furies left him not. Wherefore Apollo commanded that he should sail for the land of the Taurians and carry thence the image of Artemis and bring it to the land of the Athenians, and that after this he should have rest. Now when the two were come to the place, they saw the altar that it was red with the blood of them that had been slain thereon. And Orestes doubted how they might accomplish the things for the which he was come, for the walls of the temple were high and the gates not easy to be broken through. Therefore he would have fled to the ship, but Pylades consented not, seeing that they were not wont to go back from that to which they had set their hand, but counseled that they should hide themselves during the day in a cave that was hard by the seashore, not near to the ship, lest search should be made for them, and that by night they should creep into the temple by a space that there was between the pillars, and carry off the image, and so depart.

So they hid themselves in a cavern by the sea. But it chanced that certain herdsmen were feeding their oxen in pastures hard by the shore; one of these, coming near to the cavern, spied the young men as they sat therein, and stealing back to his fellows, said, "See ye not them that sit yonder. Surely they are gods;" for they were exceeding tall and fair to look upon. And some began to pray to them, thinking that they might be the Twin Brethren or of the sons of Nereus. But another laughed and said, "Not so; these are shipwrecked men who hide themselves, knowing that it is our custom to sacrifice strangers to our gods." To him the others gave consent and said that they should take the men prisoners that they might be sacrificed to the gods.

But while they delayed, Orestes ran forth from the cave, for the madness was come upon him, crying out, "Pylades, seest thou not that dragon from hell; and that who would kill me with the serpents of her mouth, and this again that breatheth out fire, holding my mother in her arms to cast her upon me?" And first he bellowed as a bull and then howled as a dog, for the Furies, he said, did so. But the herdsmen, when they saw this, gathered together in great fear and sat down. But when Orestes drew his sword and leapt, as a lion might leap, into the midst of the herd, slaying the beasts (for he thought in his madness that he was contending with the Furies), then the herdsmen, blowing on shells, called to the people of the land; for they feared the young men, so strong they seemed and valiant. And when no small number was gathered together, they began to cast stones and javelins at the two. And now the madness of Orestes began to abate, and Pylades tended him carefully, wiping away the foam from his mouth and holding his garments before him that he should not be wounded by the stones. But when Orestes came to himself and beheld in what straits they were, he groaned aloud and cried, "We must die, O Pylades, only let us die as befitteth brave men. Draw thy sword and follow me." And the people of the land dared not to stand before them; yet while some fled, others would cast stones at them. For all that no man wounded them. But at the last, coming about them with a great multitude, they smote the swords out of their hands with stones, and so bound them and took them to King Thoas. And the king commanded that they should be taken to the temple, that the priestess might deal with them according to the custom of the place.

So they brought the young men bound to the temple. Now the name of the one they knew, for they had heard his companion call to him, but the name of the other they knew not. And when Iphigenia saw them, she bade the people loose their bonds, for that being holy to the goddess they were free. And then—for she took the two for brothers—she asked them, saying, "Who is your mother and your father and your sister, if a sister you have? She will be bereaved of noble brothers this day. And whence come ye?"

To her Orestes answered, "What meanest thou, lady, by lamenting in this fashion over us? I hold it folly in him who must die that he should bemoan himself. Pity us not; we know what manner of sacrifices ye have in this land."

"Tell me now, which of ye two is called Pylades?"

"Not I, but this my companion."

"Of what city in the land of Greece are ye? And are ye brothers born of one mother?"

"Brothers we are, but in friendship, not in blood."

"And what is thy name?"

"That I tell thee not. Thou hast power over my body, but not over my name."

"Wilt thou not tell me thy country?"

And when he told her that his country was Argos, she asked him many things, as about Troy, and Helen, and Calchas the prophet, and Ulysses; and at last she said, "And Achilles, son of Thetis of the sea, is he yet alive?"

"He is dead and his marriage that was made at Aulis is of no effect."

"A false marriage it was, as some know full well."

"Who art thou that inquirest thus about matters in Greece?"

"I am of the land of Greece and was brought thence yet being a child. But there was a certain Agamemnon, son of Atreus; what of him?"

"I know not. Lady, leave all talk of him."

"Say not so; but do me a pleasure and tell me."

"He is dead."

"Woe is me! How died he?"

"What meaneth thy sorrow? Art thou of his kindred?"

"'Tis a pity to think how great he was, and now he hath perished."

"He was slain in a most miserable fashion by a woman, but ask no more."

"Only this one thing. Is his wife yet alive?"

"Nay; for the son whom she bare slew her, taking vengeance for his father."

"A dreadful deed, but righteous withal."

"Righteous indeed he is, but the gods love him not."

"And did the king leave any other child behind him?"

"One daughter, Electra by name."

"And is his son yet alive?"

"He is alive, but no man more miserable."

Now when Iphigenia heard that he was alive and knew that she had been deceived by the dreams which she had dreamt, she conceived a thought in her heart and said to Orestes, "Hearken now, for I have somewhat to say to thee that shall bring profit both to thee and to me. Wilt thou, if I save thee from this death, carry tidings of me to Argos to my friends and bear a tablet from me to them? For such a tablet I have with me, which one who was brought captive to this place wrote for me, pitying me, for he knew that I caused not his death, but the law of the goddess in this place. Nor have I yet found a man who should carry this thing to Argos. But thou, I judge, art of noble birth and knowest the city and those with whom I would have communication. Take then this tablet and thy life as a reward, and let this man be sacrificed to the goddess."

Then Orestes made answer, "Thou hast said well, lady, save in one thing only. That this man should be sacrificed in my stead pleaseth me not at all. For I am he that brought this voyage to pass; and this man came with me that he might help me in my troubles. Wherefore it would be a grievous wrong that he should suffer in my stead and I escape. Give then the tablet to him. He shall take it to the city of Argos and thou shalt have what thou wilt. But as for me, let them slay me if they will."

"'Tis well spoken, young man. Thou art come, I know, of a noble stock. The gods grant that my brother—for I have a brother, though he be far hence—may be such as thou. It shall be as thou wilt. This man shall depart with the tablet and thou shalt die."

Then Orestes would know the manner of the death by which he must die. And she told him that she slew not the victims with her own hand, but that there were ministers in the temple appointed to this office, she preparing them for sacrifice beforehand. Also she said that his body would be burned with fire.

And when Orestes had wished that the hand of his sister might pay due honor to him in his death, she said, "This may not be, for she is far away from this strange land. But yet, seeing that thou art a man of Argos, I myself will adorn thy tomb and pour oil of olives and honey on thy ashes." Then she departed, that she might fetch the tablet from her dwelling, bidding the attendants keep the young men fast, but without bonds.

But when she was gone, Orestes said to Pylades, "Pylades, what thinkest thou? Who is this maiden? She had great knowledge of things in Troy and Argos, and of Calchas the wise soothsayer, and of Achilles and the rest. And she made lamentation over King Agamemnon. She must be of Argos."

And Pylades answered, "This I cannot say; all men have knowledge of what befell the king. But hearken to this. It were shame to me to live if thou diest. I sailed with thee and will die with thee. For otherwise men will account lightly of me both in Argos and in Phocis, which is my own land, thinking that I betrayed thee or basely slew thee, that I might have thy kingdom, marrying thy sister, who shall inherit it in thy stead. Not so: I will die with thee and my body shall be burnt together with thine."

But Orestes answered, "I must bear my own troubles. This indeed would be a shameful thing, that when thou seekest to help me I should destroy thee. But as for me, seeing how the gods deal with me, it is well that I should die. Thou, indeed, art happy, and thy house is blessed; but my house is accursed. Go, therefore, and my sister, whom I have given thee to wife, shall bear thee children, and the house of my father shall not perish. And I charge thee that when thou art safe returned to the city of Argos, thou do these things. First, thou shalt build a tomb for me, and my sister shall make an offering there of her hair and of her tears also. And tell her that I died, slain by a woman of Argos that offered me as an offering to her gods; and I charge thee that thou leave not my sister, but be faithful to her. And now farewell, true friend and companion in my toils; for indeed I die, and Phœbus hath lied unto me, prophesying falsely."

And Pylades swore to him that he would build him a tomb and be a true husband to his sister. After this Iphigenia came forth, holding a tablet in her hand. And she said, "Here is the tablet of which I spake. But I fear lest he to whom I shall give it shall haply take no account of it when he is returned to the land. Therefore I would fain bind him with an oath that he will deliver it to them that should have it in the city of Argos." And Orestes consented, saying that she also should bind herself with an oath that she would deliver one of the two from death. So she sware by Artemis that she would persuade the king, and deliver Pylades from death. And Pylades sware on his part by Zeus, the father of heaven, that he would give the tablet to those whom it should concern. And having sworn it, he said, "But what if a storm overtake me and the tablet be lost and I only be saved?"

"I will tell thee what hath been written in the tablet; and if it perish, thou shalt tell them again; but if not, then thou shalt give it as I bid thee."

"And to whom shall I give it?"

"Thou shalt give it to Orestes, son of Agamemnon. And that which is written therein is this: 'I that was sacrificed in Aulis, even Iphigenia, who am alive and yet dead to my own people, bid thee—'"

But when Orestes heard this, he brake in, "Where is this Iphigenia? Hath the dead come back among the living?"

"Thou seest her in me. But interrupt me not. 'I bid thee fetch me before I die to Argos from a strange land, taking me from the altar that is red with the blood of strangers, whereat I serve.' And if Orestes ask by what means I am alive, thou shalt say that Artemis put a hind in my stead, and that the priest, thinking that he smote me with the knife, slew the beast, and that the goddess brought me to this land."

Then said Pylades, "My oath is easy to keep. Orestes, take thou this tablet from thy sister."

Then Orestes embraced his sister, crying—for she turned from him, not knowing what she should think—"O my sister, turn not from me; for I am thy brother whom thou didst not think to see."

And when she yet doubted, he told her of certain things by which she might know him to be Orestes—how that she had woven a tapestry wherein was set forth the strife between Atreus and Thyestes concerning the golden lamb; and that she had given a lock of her hair at Aulis to be a memorial of her; and that there was laid in her chamber at Argos the ancient spear of Pelops, her father's grandsire, with which he slew Œnomaüs and won Hippodamia to be his wife.

And when she heard this, she knew that he was indeed Orestes, whom, being an infant and the latest born of his mother, she had in time past held in her arms. But when the two had talked together for a space, rejoicing over each other and telling the things that had befallen them, Pylades said, "Greetings of friends after long parting are well; but we must needs consider how best we shall escape from this land of the barbarians."

But Iphigenia answered, "Yet nothing shall hinder me from knowing how fareth my sister Electra."

"She is married," said Orestes, "to this Pylades, whom thou seest."

"And of what country is he and who is his father?"

"His father is Strophius the Phocian; and he is a kinsman, for his mother was the daughter of Atreus and a friend also such as none other is to me."

Then Orestes set forth to his sister the cause of his coming to the land of the Taurians. And he said, "Now help me in this, my sister, that we may bear away the image of the goddess; for so doing I shall be quit of my madness, and thou wilt be brought to thy native country and the house of thy father shall prosper. But if we do it not, then shall we perish altogether."

And Iphigenia doubted much how this thing might be done. But at the last she said, "I have a device whereby I shall compass the matter. I will say that thou art come hither, having murdered thy mother, and that thou canst not be offered for a sacrifice till thou art purified with the water of the sea. Also that thou hast touched the image, and that this also must be purified in like manner. And the image I myself will bear to the sea; for, indeed, I only may touch it with my hands. And of this Pylades also I will say that he is polluted in like manner with thee. So shall we three win our way to the ship. And that this be ready it will be thy care to provide."

And when she had so said, she prayed to Artemis: "Great goddess, that didst bring me safe in days past from Aulis, bring me now also, and these that are with me, safe to the land of Greece, so that men may count thy brother Apollo to be a true prophet. Nor shouldst thou be unwilling to depart from this barbarous land and to dwell in the fair city of Athens."

After this came King Thoas, inquiring whether they had offered the strangers for sacrifice and had duly burnt their bodies with fire. To him Iphigenia made answer, "These were unclean sacrifices that thou broughtest to me, O King."

"How didst thou learn this?"

"The image of the goddess turned upon her place of her own accord and covered also her face with her hands."

"What wickedness, then, had these strangers wrought?"

"They slew their mother and had been banished therefor from the land of Greece."

"O monstrous! Such deeds we barbarians never do. And now what dost thou purpose?"

"We must purify these strangers before we offer them for a sacrifice."

"With water from the river, or in the sea?"

"In the sea. The sea cleanseth away all that is evil among men."

"Well, thou hast it here, by the very walls of the temple."

"Aye, but I must seek a place apart from men."

"So be it; go where thou wilt; I would not look on things forbidden."

"The image also must be purified."

"Surely, if the pollution from these murderers of their mother hath touched it. This is well thought of in thee."

Then she instructed the king that he should bring the strangers out of the temple, having first bound them and veiled their heads. Also that certain of his guards should go with her, but that all the people of the city should be straitly commanded to stay within doors, that so they might not be defiled; and that he himself should abide in the temple and purify it with fire, covering his head with his garments when the strangers should pass by. "And be not troubled," she said, "if I seem to be long doing these things."

"Take what time thou wilt," he said, "so that thou do all things in order."

So certain of the king's guards brought the two young men from out of the temple, and Iphigenia led them towards the place where the ship of Orestes lay at anchor. But when they were come near to the shore, she bade them halt nor come over-near, for that she had that to do in which they must have no part. And she took the chain wherewith the young men were bound in her hands and set up a strange song as of one that sought enchantments. And after that the guards sat where she bade them for a long time, they began to fear lest the strangers should have slain the priestess and so fled. Yet they moved not, fearing to see that which was forbidden. But at the last with one consent they rose up. And when they were come to the sea, they saw the ship trimmed to set forth, and fifty sailors on the benches having oars in their hands ready for rowing; and the two young men were standing unbound upon the shore near to the stern. And other sailors were dragging the ship by the cable to the shore that the young men might embark. Then the guards laid hold of the rudder and sought to take it from its place, crying, "Who are ye that carry away priestesses and the images of our gods?" Then Orestes said, "I am Orestes, and I carry away my sister." But the guards laid hold of Iphigenia; and when the sailors saw this they leapt from the ship; and neither the one nor the other had swords in their hands, but they fought with their fists and their feet also. And as the sailors were strong and skilful, the king's men were driven back sorely bruised and wounded. And when they fled to a bank that was hard by and cast stones at the ship, the archers standing on the stern shot at them with arrows. Then—for his sister feared to come farther—Orestes leapt into the sea and raised her upon his shoulder and so lifted her into the ship, and the image of the goddess with her. And Pylades cried, "Lay hold of your oars, ye sailors, and smite the sea, for we have that for the which we came to this land." So the sailors rowed with all their might; and while the ship was in the harbor it went well with them, but when it was come to the open sea a great wave took it, for a violent wind blew against it and drove it backwards to the shore.

And one of the guards when he saw this ran to King Thoas and told him, and the king made haste and sent messengers mounted upon horses, to call the men of the land that they might do battle with Orestes and his comrade. But while he was yet sending them, there appeared in the air above his head the goddess Athene, who spake, saying, "Cease, King Thoas, from pursuing this man and his companions; for he hath come hither on this errand by the command of Apollo; and I have persuaded Poseidon that he make the sea smooth for him to depart."

And King Thoas answered, "It shall be as thou wilt, O goddess; and though Orestes hath borne away his sister and the image, I dismiss my anger, for who can fight against the gods?"

So Orestes departed and came to his own country and dwelt in peace, being set free from his madness, according to the word of Apollo.

The Sack Of Troy

For ten years King Agamemnon and the men of Greece laid siege to Troy. But though sentence had gone forth against the city, yet the day of its fall tarried, because certain of the gods loved it well and defended it, as Apollo and Mars, the god of war, and Father Jupiter himself. Wherefore Minerva put it into the heart of Epeius, Lord of the Isles, that he should make a cunning device wherewith to take the city. Now the device was this: he made a great horse of wood, feigning it to be a peace-offering to Minerva, that the Greeks might have a safe return to their homes. In the belly of this there hid themselves certain of the bravest of the chiefs, as Menelaüs, and Ulysses, and Thoas the Ætolian, and Machaon the great physician, and Pyrrhus, son of Achilles (but Achilles himself was dead, slain by Paris, Apollo helping, even as he was about to take the city), and others also, and with them Epeius himself. But the rest of the people made as if they had departed to their homes; only they went not further than Tenedos, which was an island near to the coast.

Great joy was there in Troy when it was noised abroad that the men of Greece had departed. The gates were opened, and the people went forth to see the plain and the camp. And one said to another as they went, "Here they set the battle in array, and there were the tents of the fierce Achilles, and there lay the ships." And some stood and marveled at the great peace-offering to Minerva, even the horse of wood. And Thymœtes, who was one of the elders of the city, was the first who advised that it should be brought within the walls and set in the citadel. Now whether he gave this counsel out of a false heart or because the gods would have it so, no man knows. But Capys, and others with him, said that it should be drowned in water or burned with fire, or that men should pierce it and see whether there were aught within. And the people were divided, some crying one thing and some another. Then came forward the priest Laocoön, and a great company with him, crying, "What madness is this? Think ye that the men of Greece are indeed departed or that there is any profit in their gifts? Surely there are armed men in this mighty horse; or haply they have made it that they may look down upon our walls. Touch it not, for as for these men of Greece, I fear them, even though they bring gifts in their hands."

And as he spake he cast his great spear at the horse, so that it sounded again. But the gods would not that Troy should be saved.

Meanwhile there came certain shepherds dragging with them one whose hands were bound behind his back. He had come forth to them, they said, of his own accord when they were in the field. And first the young men gathered about him mocking him, but when he cried aloud, "What place is left for me, for the Greeks suffer me not to live and the men of Troy cry for vengeance upon me?" they rather pitied him, and bade him speak and say whence he came and what he had to tell.

Then the man spake, turning to King Priam: "I will speak the truth, whatever befall me. My name is Sinon and I deny not that I am a Greek. Haply thou hast heard the name of Palamedes, whom the Greeks slew, but now, being dead, lament; and the cause was that because he counseled peace, men falsely accused him of treason. Now, of this Palamedes I was a poor kinsman and followed him to Troy. And when he was dead, through the false witness of Ulysses, I lived in great grief and trouble, nor could I hold my peace, but sware that if ever I came back to Argos I would avenge me of him that had done this deed. Then did Ulysses seek occasion against me, whispering evil things, nor rested till at the last, Calchas the soothsayer helping him — but what profit it that I should tell these things? For doubtless ye hold one Greek to be even as another. Wherefore slay me and doubtless ye will do a pleasure to Ulysses and the sons of Atreus."

Then they bade him tell on, and he said:

"Often would the Greeks have fled to their homes, being weary of the war, but still the stormy sea hindered them. And when this horse that ye see had been built, most of all did the dreadful thunder roll from the one end of the heaven to the other. Then the Greeks sent one who should inquire of Apollo; and Apollo answered them thus: 'Men of Greece, even as ye appeased the winds with blood when ye came to Troy, so must ye appease them with blood now that ye would go from thence.' Then did men tremble to think on whom the doom should fall, and Ulysses, with much clamor, drew forth Calchas the soothsayer into the midst, and bade him say who it was that the gods would have as a sacrifice. Then did many forbode evil for me. Ten days did the soothsayer keep silence, saying that he would not give any man to death. But then, for in truth the two had planned the matter beforehand, he spake, appointing me to die. And to this thing they all agreed, each being glad to turn to another that which he feared for himself. But when the day was come and all things were ready, the salted meal for the sacrifice and the garlands, lo! I burst my bonds and fled and hid myself in the sedges of a pool, waiting till they should have set sail, if haply that might be. But never shall I see country or father or children again. For doubtless on these will they take vengeance for my flight. Only do thou, O King, have pity on me, who have suffered many things, not having harmed any man."

And King Priam had pity on him, and bade them loose his bonds, saying, "Whoever thou art, forget now thy country. Henceforth thou art one of us. But tell me true: why made they this huge horse? Who contrived it? What seek they by it—to please the gods or to further their siege?"

Then said Sinon, and as he spake he stretched his hands to the sky, "I call you to witness, ye everlasting fires of heaven, that with good right I now break my oath of fealty and reveal the secrets of my countrymen. Listen then, O King. All our hope has ever been in the help of Minerva. But from the day when Diomed and Ulysses dared, having bloody hands, to snatch her image from her holy place in Troy, her face was turned from us. Well do I remember how the eyes of the image, well-nigh before they had set it in the camp, blazed with wrath, and how the salt sweat stood upon its limbs, aye, and how it thrice leapt from the ground, shaking shield and spear. Then Calchas told us that we must cross the seas again and seek at home fresh omens for our war. And this, indeed, they are doing even now, and will return anon. Also the soothsayer said, 'Meanwhile ye must make the likeness of a horse, to be a peace-offering to Minerva. And take heed that ye make it huge of bulk, so that the men of Troy may not receive it into their gates, nor bring it within their walls and get safety for themselves thereby. For if,' he said, 'the men of Troy harm this image at all, they shall surely perish; but if they bring it into their city, then shall Asia lay siege hereafter to the city of Pelops, and our children shall suffer the doom which we would fain have brought on Troy.'"

These words wrought much on the men of Troy, and as they pondered on them, lo! the gods sent another marvel to deceive them. For while Laocoön, the priest of Neptune, was slaying a bull at the altar of his god, there came two serpents across the sea from Tenedos, whose heads and necks, whereon were thick manes of hair, were high above the waves, and many scaly coils trailed behind in the waters. And when they reached the land they still sped forward. Their eyes were red as blood and blazed with fire and their forked tongues hissed loud for rage. Then all the men of Troy grew pale with fear and fled away, but these turned not aside this way or that, seeking Laocoön where he stood. And first they wrapped themselves about his little sons, one serpent about each, and began to devour them. And when the father would have given help to his children, having a sword in his hand, they seized upon himself and bound him fast with their folds. Twice they compassed him about his body, and twice about his neck, lifting their heads far above him. And all the while he strove to tear them away with his hands, his priest's garlands dripping with blood. Nor did he cease to cry horribly aloud, even as a bull bellows when after an ill stroke of the axe it flees from the altar. But when their work was done, the two glided to the citadel of Minerva and hid themselves beneath the feet and the shield of the goddess. And men said one to another, "Lo! the priest Laocoön has been judged according to his deeds; for he cast his spear against this holy thing, and now the gods have slain him." Then all cried out together that the horse of wood must be drawn to the citadel. Whereupon they opened the Scæan Gate and pulled down the wall that was thereby, and put rollers under the feet of the horse and joined ropes thereto. So in much joy they drew it into the city, youths and maidens singing about it the while and laying their hands to the ropes with great gladness. And yet there wanted no signs and tokens of evil to come. Four times it halted on the threshold of the gate, and men might have heard a clashing of arms within. Cassandra also opened her mouth, prophesying evil; but no man heeded her, for that was ever the doom upon her, not to be believed, though speaking truth. So the men of Troy drew the horse into the city. And that night they kept a feast to all the gods with great joy not knowing that the last day of the great city had come.

But when night was now fully come and the men of Troy lay asleep, lo! from the ship of King Agamemnon there rose up a flame for a signal to the Greeks; and these straightway manned their ships and made across the sea from Tenedos, there being a great calm and the moon also giving them light. Sinon likewise opened a secret door that was in the great horse and the chiefs issued forth therefrom and opened the gates of the city, slaying those that kept watch.

Meanwhile there came a vision to Æneas, who now, Hector being dead, was the chief hope and stay of the men of Troy. It was Hector's self that he seemed to see, but not such as he had seen him coming back rejoicing with the arms of Achilles or setting fire to the ships, but even as he lay after that Achilles dragged him at his chariot wheels, covered with dust, and blood, his feet swollen and pierced through with thongs. To him said Æneas, not knowing what he said, "Why hast thou tarried so long? Much have we suffered waiting for thee! And what grief hath marked thy face, and whence these wounds?"

But to this the spirit answered nothing, but said, groaning the while, "Fly, son of Venus, fly and save thee from these flames. The enemy is in the walls and Troy hath utterly perished. If any hand could have saved our city, this hand had done so. Thou art now the hope of Troy. Take then her gods and flee with them for company, seeking the city that thou shalt one day build across the sea."

And now the alarm of battle came nearer and nearer, and Æneas, waking from sleep, climbed upon the roof and looked on the city. As a shepherd stands and sees a fierce flame sweeping before the south wind over the corn-fields or a flood rushing down from the mountains, so he stood. And as he looked, the great palace of Deïphobus sank down in the fire and the house of Ucalegon that was hard by, blazed forth, till the sea by Sigeüm shone with the light. Then, scarce knowing what he sought, he girded on his armor, thinking perchance that he might yet win some place of vantage or at the least might avenge himself on the enemy or find honor in his death. But as he passed from out of his house there met him Panthus, the priest of Apollo that was on the citadel, who cried to him, "O Æneas, the glory is departed from Troy and the Greeks have the mastery in the city; for armed men are coming forth from the great horse of wood and thousands also swarm in at the gates, which Sinon hath treacherously opened." And as he spake others came up under the light of the moon, as Hypanis and Dymas and young Corœbus, who had but newly come to Troy, seeking Cassandra to be his wife. To whom Æneas spake: "If ye are minded, my brethren, to follow me to the death, come on. For how things fare this night ye see. The gods who were the stay of this city have departed from it; nor is aught remaining to which we may bring succor. Yet can we die as brave men in battle. And haply he that counts his life to be lost may yet save it." Then, even as ravening wolves hasten through the mist seeking for prey, so they went through the city, doing dreadful deeds. And for a while the men of Greece fled before them.

First of all there met them Androgeos with a great company following him, who, thinking them to be friends, said, "Haste, comrades; why are ye so late? We are spoiling this city of Troy and ye are but newly come from the ships." But forthwith, for they answered him not as he had looked for, he knew that he had fallen among enemies. Then even as one who treads upon a snake unawares among thorns and flies from it when it rises angrily against him with swelling neck, so Androgeos would have fled. But the men of Troy rushed on and, seeing that they knew all the place and that great fear was upon the Greeks, slew many men. Then said Corœbus, "We have good luck in this matter, my friends. Come now, let us change our shields and put upon us the armor of these Greeks. For whether we deal with our enemy by craft or by force, who will ask?" Then he took to himself the helmet and shield of Androgeos and also girded the sword upon him. In like manner did the others, and thus, going disguised among the Greeks, slew many, so that some again fled to the ships and some were fain to climb into the horse of wood. But lo! men came dragging by the hair from the temple of Minerva the virgin Cassandra, whom when Corœbus beheld, and how she lifted up her eyes to heaven (but as for her hands, they were bound with iron), he endured not the sight, but threw himself upon those that dragged her, the others following him. Then did a grievous mischance befall them, for the men of Troy that stood upon the roof of the temple cast spears against them, judging them to be enemies. The Greeks also, being wroth that the virgin should be taken from them, fought the more fiercely, and many who had before been put to flight in the city came against them and prevailed, being indeed many against few. Then first of all fell Corœbus, being slain by Peneleus the Bœotian, and Rhipeus also, the most righteous of all the sons of Troy. But the gods dealt not with him after his righteousness. Hypanis also was slain and Dymas, and Panthus escaped not for all that more than other men he feared the gods and was also the priest of Apollo.

Then was Æneas severed from the rest, having with him two only, Iphitus and Pelias, Iphitus being an old man and Pelias sorely wounded by Ulysses. And these, hearing a great shouting, hastened to the palace of King Priam, where the battle was fiercer than in any place beside. For some of the Greeks were seeking to climb the walls, laying ladders thereto, whereon they stood, holding forth their shields with their left hands and with their right grasping the roofs. And the men of Troy, on the other hand, being in the last extremity, tore down the battlements and the gilded beams wherewith the men of old had adorned the palace. Then Æneas, knowing of a secret door whereby the unhappy Andromache in past days had been wont to enter, bringing her son Astyanax to his grandfather, climbed on to the roof and joined himself to those that fought therefrom. Now upon this roof there was a tower, whence all Troy could be seen and the camp of the Greeks and the ships. This the men of Troy loosened from its foundations with bars of iron, and thrust it over, so that it fell upon the enemy, slaying many of them. But not the less did others press forward, casting the while stones and javelins and all that came to their hands.

Meanwhile others sought to break down the gates of the palace, Pyrrhus, son of Achilles, being foremost among them, clad in shining armor of bronze. Like to a serpent was he, which sleeps indeed during the winter, but in the spring comes forth into the light, full-fed on evil herbs, and, having cast his skin and renewed his youth, lifts his head into the light of the sun and hisses with forked tongue. And with Pyrrhus were tall Periphas, and Automedon, who had been armor-bearer to his father Achilles, and following them the youth of Scyros, which was the kingdom of his grandfather Lycomedes. With a great battle-axe he hewed through the doors, breaking down also the door-posts, though they were plated with bronze, making, as it were, a great window, through which a man might see the palace within, the hall of King Priam and of the kings who had reigned aforetime in Troy. But when they that were within perceived it, there arose a great cry of women wailing aloud and clinging to the doors and kissing them. But ever Pyrrhus pressed on, fierce and strong as ever was his father Achilles, nor could aught stand against him, either the doors or they that guarded them. Then, as a river bursts its banks and overflows the plain, so did the sons of Greece rush into the palace.

But old Priam, when he saw the enemy in his hall, girded on him his armor, which now by reason of old age he had long laid aside, and took a spear in his hand and would have gone against the adversary, only Queen Hecuba called to him from where she sat. For she and her daughters had fled to the great altar of the household gods and sat crowded about it like unto doves that are driven by a storm. Now the altar stood in an open court that was in the midst of the palace, with a great bay-tree above it. So when she saw Priam, how he had girded himself with armor as a youth, she cried to him and said, "What hath bewitched thee, that thou girdest thyself with armor? It is not the sword that shall help us this day; no, not though my own Hector were here, but rather the gods and their altars. Come hither to us, for here thou wilt be safe, or at the least wilt die with us."

So she made the old man sit down in the midst. But lo! there came flying through the palace, Polites, his son, wounded to death by the spear of Pyrrhus, and Pyrrhus close behind him. And he, even as he came into the sight of his father and his mother, fell dead upon the ground. But when King Priam saw it he contained not himself, but cried aloud, "Now may the gods, if there be any justice in heaven, recompense thee for this wickedness, seeing that thou hast not spared to slay the son before his father's eyes. Great Achilles, whom thou falsely callest thy sire, did not thus to Priam, though he was an enemy, but reverenced right and truth and gave the body of Hector for burial and sent me back to my city."

And as he spake the old man cast a spear, but aimless and without force, which pierced not even the boss of the shield.

Then said the son of Achilles, "Go thou and tell my father of his unworthy son and all these evils deeds. And that thou mayest tell him die!" And as he spake he caught in his left hand the old man's white hair and dragged him, slipping the while in the blood of his own son, to the altar, and then, lifting his sword high for a blow, drove it to the hilt in the old man's side. So King Priam, who had ruled mightily over many peoples and countries in the land of Asia, was slain that night, having first seen Troy burning about him and his citadel laid even with the ground. So was his carcass cast out upon the earth, headless and without a name.

Beowulf And Grendel

Long ago there ruled over the Danes a king called Hrothgar. He gained success and glory in war, so that his loyal kinsmen willingly obeyed him, and everything prospered in his land.

One day it came into his mind that he would build a princely banquet-hall, where he might entertain both the young and old of his kingdom; and he had the work widely made known to many a tribe over the earth, so that they might bring rich gifts to beautify the hall.

In course of time the banquet-house was built and towered aloft, high and battlemented. Then Hrothgar gave it the name of Heorot, and called his guests to the banquet, and gave them gifts of rings and other treasures; and afterwards every day the joyous sound of revelry rang loud in the hall, with the music of the harp and the clear notes of the singers.

But it was not long before the pleasure of the king's men was broken, for a wicked demon began to work mischief against them. This cruel spirit was called Grendel, and he dwelt on the moors and among the fens. One night he came to Heorot when the noble guests lay at rest after the feast, and seizing thirty thanes as they slept, set off on his homeward journey, exulting in his booty.

At break of day his deed was known to all men, and great was the grief among the thanes. The good King Hrothgar also sat in sorrow, suffering heavy distress for the death of his warriors.

Not long afterwards Grendel again appeared, and wrought a yet worse deed of murder. After that the warriors no longer dared to sleep at Heorot, but sought out secret resting-places, leaving the great house empty.

A long time passed. For the space of twelve winters Grendel waged a perpetual feud against Hrothgar and his people; the livelong night he roamed over the misty moors, visiting Heorot, and destroying both the tried warriors and the young men whenever he was able. Hrothgar was broken-hearted, and many were the councils held in secret to deliberate what it were best to do against these fearful terrors; but nothing availed to stop the fiend's ravages.

Now the tale of Grendel's deeds went forth into many lands; and amongst those who heard of it were the Geats, whose king was Higelac. Chief of his thanes was a noble and powerful warrior named Beowulf, who resolved to go to the help of the Danes. He bade his men make ready a good sea-boat, that he might go across the wild swan's path to seek out Hrothgar and aid him; and his people encouraged him to go on that dangerous errand even though he was dear to them.

So Beowulf chose fourteen of his keenest warriors, and sailed away over the waves in his well-equipped vessel, till he came within sight of the cliffs and mountains of Hrothgar's kingdom. The Danish warder, who kept guard over the coast, saw them as they were making their ship fast and carrying their bright weapons on shore. So he mounted his horse and rode to meet them, bearing in his hand his staff of office; and he questioned them closely as to whence they came and what their business was.

Then Beowulf explained their errand, and the warder, when he had heard it, bade them pass onwards, bearing their weapons, and gave orders that their ship should be safely guarded.

Soon they came within sight of the fair palace Heorot, and the warder showed them the way to Hrothgar's court, and then bade them farewell, and returned to keep watch upon the coast.

Then the bold thanes marched forward to Heorot, their armor and their weapons glittering as they went. Entering the hall, they set their shields and bucklers against the walls, placed their spears upright in a sheaf together, and sat down on the benches, weary with their seafaring.

Then a proud liegeman of Hrothgar's stepped forward and asked:

"Whence bring ye your shields, your gray war-shirts and frowning helmets, and this sheaf of spears? Never saw I men of more valiant aspect."

"We are Higelac's boon companions," answered Beowulf. "Beowulf is my name, and I desire to declare my errand to the great prince, thy lord, if he will grant us leave to approach him."

So Wulfgar, another of Hrothgar's chieftains, went out to the king where he sat with the assembly of his earls and told him of the arrival of the strangers, and Hrothgar received the news with joy, for he had known Beowulf when he was a boy, and had heard of his fame as a warrior. Therefore he bade Wulfgar bring him to his presence, and soon Beowulf stood before him and cried:

"Hail to thee, Hrothgar! I have heard the tale of Grendel, and my people, who know my strength and prowess, have counseled me to seek thee out. For I have wrought great deeds in the past, and now I shall do battle against this monster. Men say that so thick is his tawny hide that no weapon can injure him. I therefore disdain to carry sword or shield into the combat, but will fight with the strength of my arm only, and either I will conquer the fiend or he will bear away my dead body to the moor. Send to Higelac, if I fall in the fight, my beautiful breastplate. I have no fear of death, for Destiny must ever be obeyed."

Then Hrothgar told Beowulf of the great sorrow caused to him by Grendel's terrible deeds, and of the failure of all the attempts that had been made by the warriors to overcome him;

and afterwards he bade him sit down with his followers to partake of a meal.

So a bench was cleared for the Geats, and a thane waited upon them, and all the noble warriors gathered together, and a great feast was held once more in Heorot with song and revelry. Waltheow, Hrothgar's queen, came forth also, and handed the wine-cup to each of the thanes, pledging the king in joyful mood and thanking Beowulf for his offer of help.

At last all the company arose to go to rest; and Hrothgar entrusted the guardianship of Heorot to Beowulf with cheering words, and so bade him good night. Then all left the hall, save only a watch appointed by Hrothgar, and Beowulf himself with his followers, who laid themselves down to rest.

No long time passed before Grendel came prowling from his home on the moors under the misty slopes. Full of his evil purpose, he burst with fury into the hall and strode forward raging, a hideous, fiery light gleaming from his eyes. In the hall lay the warriors asleep, and Grendel laughed in his heart as he gazed at them, thinking to feast upon them all. Quickly he seized a sleeping warrior and devoured him; then, stepping forward, he reached out his hand towards Beowulf as he lay at rest.

But the hero was ready for him, and seized his arm in a deadly grip such as Grendel had never felt before. Terror arose in the monster's heart, and his mind was bent on flight; but he could not get away.

Then Beowulf stood upright and grappled with him firmly, and the two rocked to and fro in the struggle, knocking over benches and shaking the hall with the violence of their fight. Suddenly a new and terrible cry arose, the cry of Grendel in fear and pain, for never once did Beowulf relax his hold upon him. Then many of Beowulf's earls drew their swords and rushed to aid their master; but no blade could pierce him and nothing but Beowulf's mighty strength could prevail.

At last the monster's arm was torn off at the shoulder, and sick unto death, he fled to the fens, there to end his joyless life.

Then Beowulf rejoiced at his night's work, wherein he had freed Heorot forever from the fiend's ravages.

Now on the morrow the warriors flocked to the hall; and when they heard what had taken place, they went out and followed Grendel's tracks to a mere upon the moors, into which he had plunged and given up his life. Then, sure of his death, they returned rejoicing to Heorot, talking of Beowulf's glorious deed; and there they found the king and queen and a great company of people awaiting them.

And now there was great rejoicing and happiness. Fair and gracious were the thanks that Hrothgar gave to Beowulf, and great was the feast prepared in Heorot. Cloths embroidered with gold were hung along the walls and the hall was decked in every possible way.

When all were seated at the feast, Hrothgar bade the attendants bring forth his gifts to Beowulf as a reward of victory. He gave him an embroidered banner, a helmet and breastplate, and a valuable sword, all adorned with gold and richly ornamented. Also he gave orders to the servants to bring into the court eight horses, on one of which was a curiously adorned and very precious saddle, which the king was wont to use himself when he rode to practice the sword-game. These also he gave to Beowulf, thus like a true man requiting his valiant deeds with horses and other precious gifts. He bestowed treasures also on each of Beowulf's followers and gave orders that a price should be paid in gold for the man whom the wicked Grendel had slain.

After this there arose within the hall the din of voices and the sound of song; the instruments also were brought out and Hrothgar's minstrel sang a ballad for the delight of the warriors. Waltheow too came forth, bearing in her train presents for Beowulf—a cup, two armlets, raiment and rings, and the largest and richest collar that could be found in all the world.

Now when evening came Hrothgar departed to his rest, and the warriors cleared the hall and lay down to sleep once more, with their shields and armor beside them as was their custom. But Beowulf was not with them, for another resting-place had been assigned to him that night, for all thought that there was now no longer any danger to be feared.

But in this they were mistaken, as they soon learnt to their cost. For no sooner were they all asleep than Grendel's mother, a monstrous witch who dwelt at the bottom of a cold mere, came to Heorot to avenge her son and burst into the hall. The thanes started up in terror, hastily grasping their swords; but she seized upon Asher, the most beloved of Hrothgar's warriors, who still lay sleeping, and bore him off with her to the fens, carrying also with her Grendel's arm, which lay at one end of the hall.

Then there arose an uproar and the sound of mourning in Heorot. In fierce and gloomy mood Hrothgar summoned Beowulf and told him the ghastly tale, begging him, if he dared, to go forth to seek out the monster and destroy it.

Full of courage, Beowulf answered with cheerful words, promising that Grendel's mother should not escape him; and soon he was riding forth fully equipped on his quest, accompanied by Hrothgar and many a good warrior. They were able to follow the witch's tracks right through the forest glades and across the gloomy moor, till they came to a spot where some mountain trees bent over a hoar rock, beneath which lay a dreary and troubled lake; and there beside the water's edge lay the head of Asher, and they knew that the witch must be at the bottom of the water.

Full of grief, the warriors sat down, while Beowulf arrayed himself in his cunningly fashioned coat of mail and his richly ornamented helmet. Then he turned to Hrothgar and spoke a last word to him.

"If the fight go against me, great chieftain, be thou a guardian to my thanes, my kinsmen and my trusty comrades; and send thou to Higelac those treasures that thou gavest me, that he may know thy kindness to me. Now will I earn glory for myself, or death shall take me away."

So saying, he plunged into the gloomy lake, at the bottom of which was Grendel's mother. Very soon she perceived his approach, and rushing forth, grappled with him and dragged him down to her den, where many horrible sea-beasts joined in the fight against him. This den was so fashioned that the water could not enter it, and it was lit by the light of a fire that shone brightly in the midst of it.

And now Beowulf drew his sword and thrust at his terrible foe; but the weapon could not injure her, and he was forced to fling it away and trust in the powerful grip of his arms as he had done with Grendel. Seizing the witch, he shook her till she sank down on the ground; but she quickly rose again and requited him with a terrible hand-clutch, which caused Beowulf to stagger and then fall. Throwing herself upon him, she seized a dagger to strike him; but he wrenched himself free and once more stood upright.

Then he suddenly perceived an ancient sword hanging upon the wall of the den, and seized it as a last resource. Fierce and savage, but well-nigh hopeless, he struck the monster heavily upon the neck with it. Then, to his joy, the blade pierced right through her body and she sank down dying.

At that moment the flames of the fire leapt up, throwing a brilliant light over the den; and there against the wall Beowulf beheld the dead body of Grendel lying on a couch. With one swinging blow of the powerful sword he struck off his head as a trophy to carry to Hrothgar.

But now a strange thing happened, for the blade of the sword began to melt away even as ice melts, and soon nothing was left of it save the hilt. Carrying this and Grendel's head, Beowulf now left the den and swam upwards to the surface of the lake.

There the thanes met him with great rejoicings, and some quickly helped him to undo his armor, while others prepared to carry the great head of Grendel back to Heorot. It took four men to carry it, and ghastly, though wonderful, was the sight of it.

And now once more the warriors assembled in Heorot, and Beowulf recounted to Hrothgar the full tale of his adventure and presented to him the hilt of the wonderful sword. Again the king thanked him from the depth of his heart for his valiant deeds; and as before a fair feast was prepared and the warriors made merry till night came and they repaired to rest, certain this time of their safety.

Now on the morrow Beowulf and his nobles made ready to depart to their own land; and when they were fully equipped they went to bid farewell to Hrothgar. Then Beowulf spoke, saying:

"Now are we voyagers eager to return to our lord Higelac. We have been right well and heartily entertained, O king, and if there is aught further that I can ever do for thee, then I shall be ready for thy service. If ever I hear that thy neighbors are again persecuting thee, I will bring a thousand thanes to thy aid; and I know that Higelac will uphold me in this."

"Dear are thy words to me, O Beowulf," Hrothgar made answer, "and great is thy wisdom. If Fate should take away the life of Higelac, the Geats could have no better king than thou; and hereafter there shall never more be feuds between the Danes and the Geats, for thou by thy great deeds hast made a lasting bond of friendship between them."

Then Hrothgar gave more gifts to Beowulf and bade him seek his beloved people and afterwards come back again to visit him, for so dearly had he grown to love him that he longed to see him again.

So the two embraced and bade each other farewell with great affection, and then at last Beowulf went down to where his ship rode at anchor and sailed away with his followers to his own country, taking with him the many gifts that Hrothgar had made to him. And coming to Higelac's court, he told him of his adventures, and having shown him the treasure, gave it all up to him, so loyal and true was he. But Higelac in return gave Beowulf a goodly sword and seven thousand pieces of gold and a manor-house, also a princely seat for him to dwell in. There Beowulf lived in peace, and not for many years was he called to fresh adventures.

Beowulf and the Fire-Dragon

After his return to the land of the Geats, Beowulf served Higelac faithfully till the day of the king's death, which befell in an expedition that he made to Friesland. Beowulf was with him on that disastrous journey, and only with difficulty did he escape with his life. But when he returned as a poor solitary fugitive to his people, Hygd, Higelac's wife, offered him the kingdom and the king's treasures, for she feared that her young son Heardred was not strong enough to hold the throne of his fathers against invading foes.

Beowulf, however, would not accept the kingdom, but rather chose to uphold Heardred among the people, giving him friendly counsel and serving him faithfully and honorably.

But before very long Heardred was killed in battle, and then at last Beowulf consented to become king of the Geats.

For fifty years he ruled well and wisely and his people prospered. But at last trouble came in the ravages of a terrible dragon, and once more Beowulf was called forth to a terrific combat.

For three hundred years this dragon had kept watch over a hoard of treasure on a mountain by the seashore in the country of the Geats. The treasure had been hidden in a cave under the mountain by a band of sea-robbers; and when the last of them was dead the dragon took possession of the cave and of the treasure and kept fierce watch over them.

But one day a poor man came to the spot while the dragon was fast asleep and carried off part of the treasure to his master.

When the dragon awoke he soon discovered the man's footprints, and on examining the cave he found that part of the gold and splendid jewels had disappeared. In wrathful and savage mood he sought all round the mountain for the robber, but could find no one.

So when evening came he went forth eager for revenge, and throwing out flashes of fire in every direction, he began to set fire to all the land. Beowulf's own princely manor-house was burnt down and terrible destruction was wrought on every hand, till day broke and the fire-dragon returned to his den.

Great was Beowulf's grief at this dire misfortune, and eager was his desire for vengeance. He scorned to seek the foe with a great host behind him, nor did he dread the combat in any way, for he called to mind his many feats of war, and especially his fight with Grendel.

So he quickly had fashioned a mighty battle-shield, made entirely of iron, for he knew that the wooden one that he was wont to use would be burnt up by the flames of the fire-dragon. Then he chose out eleven of his earls, and together they set out for the mountain, led thither by the man who had stolen the treasure.

When they came to the mouth of the cave Beowulf bade farewell to his companions, for he was resolved to fight single-handed against the foe.

"Many a fight have I fought in my youth," he said, "and now once more will I, the guardian of my people, seek the combat. I would not bear any sword or other weapon against the dragon if I thought that I could grapple with him as I did with the monster Grendel. But I fear that I shall not be able to approach so close to this foe, for he will send forth hot, raging fire and venomous breath. Yet am I resolute in mood, fearless and resolved not to yield one foot's-breadth to the monster.

"Tarry ye here on the hill, my warriors, and watch which of us two will survive the deadly combat, for this is no enterprise for you. I only can attempt it, because such great strength has been given to me. Therefore I will do battle alone and will either slay the dragon and win the treasure for my people or fall in the fight, as destiny shall appoint."

When he had spoken thus Beowulf strode forward to the fight, armed with his iron shield, his sword and his dagger. A stone arch spanned the mouth of the cave, and on one side a boiling stream, hot as though with raging fires, rushed forth. Undaunted by it, Beowulf uttered a shout to summon the dragon to the fight. Immediately a burning breath from the monster came out of the rock, the earth rumbled and then the dragon rushed forth to meet his fate.

Standing with his huge shield held well before him, Beowulf received the attack and struck from beneath his shield at the monster's side. But his blade failed him and turned aside, and the blow but served to enrage the dragon, so that he darted forth such blasting rays of deadly fire that Beowulf was well nigh overwhelmed and the fight went hard with him.

Now his eleven chosen comrades could see the combat from where they stood; and one of them, Beowulf's kinsman Wiglaf, was moved to great sorrow at the sight of his lord's distress. At last he could bear it no longer, but grasped his wooden shield and his sword and cried to the other thanes:

"Remember how we promised our lord in the banquet-hall, when he gave us our helmets and swords and battle-gear, that we would one day repay him for his gifts. Now is the day come that our liege lord has need of the strength of good warriors. We must go help him, even though he thought to accomplish this mighty work alone, for we can never return to our homes if we have not slain the enemy and saved our king's life. Rather than live when he is dead, I will perish with him in this deadly fire."

Then he rushed through the noisome smoke to his lord's side, crying:

"Dear Beowulf, take courage. Remember thy boast that thy valor shall never fail thee in thy lifetime, and defend thyself now with all thy might, and I will help thee."

But the other warriors were afraid to follow him, so that Beowulf and Wiglaf stood alone to face the dragon.

As soon as the monster advanced upon them, Wiglaf's wooden shield was burnt away by the flames, so that he was forced to take refuge behind Beowulf's iron shield; and this time when Beowulf struck with his sword, it was shivered to pieces. Then the dragon flung himself upon him and caught him up in his arms, crushing him till he lay senseless and covered with wounds.

But now Wiglaf showed his valor and strength, and smote the monster with such mighty blows that at last the fire coming forth from him began to abate somewhat. Then Beowulf came once more to his senses, and drawing his deadly knife, struck with it from beneath; and at last the force of the blows from the two noble kinsmen felled the fierce fire-dragon and he sank down dead beside them.

But Beowulf's wounds were very great, and he knew that the joys of life were ended for him and that death was very near. So while Wiglaf with wonderful tenderness unfastened his helmet for him and refreshed him with water, he spoke, saying:

"Though I am sick with mortal wounds, there is yet some comfort remaining for me. For I have governed my people for fifty winters and kept them safe from invading foes; yet have not sought out quarrels nor led my kinsmen to dire slaughter when there was no need. Therefore the Ruler of all men will not blame me when my life departs from my body.

"And now go thou quickly, dear Wiglaf, to spy out the treasure within the cave, so that I may see what wealth I have won for my people before I die."

So Wiglaf went into the cave and there he saw many precious jewels, old vessels, helmets, gold armlets and other treasures, which excelled in beauty and number any that mankind has ever known. Moreover, high above the treasure flapped a marvelous gilded standard, from which came a ray of light which lit up all the cave.

Then Wiglaf seized as much as he could carry of the precious spoils, and taking the standard also, hastened back to his lord, dreading lest he should find him already dead.

Beowulf was very near his life's end, but when Wiglaf had again revived him with water, he had strength to speak once more.

"Glad am I," he said, "that I have been able before my death to gain so much for my people. But now I may no longer abide here. Bid the gallant warriors burn my body on the headland here which juts into the sea, and afterwards raise a huge mound on the same spot, that the sailors who drive their vessels over the misty floods may call it Beowulf's Mound."

Then the dauntless prince undid the golden collar from his neck and gave it to Wiglaf with his helmet and coat of mail, saying:

"Thou art the last of all our race, for Fate has swept away all my kindred save thee to their doom, and now I also must join them," and with these words the aged king fell back dead.

Now as Wiglaf sat by his lord, grieving sorely at his death, the other ten thanes who had shown themselves to be faithless and cowardly approached with shame to his side. Then Wiglaf turned to them, crying bitterly:

"Truly our liege lord flung away utterly in vain the battle-gear that he gave ye. Little could he boast of his comrades when the hour of need came. I myself was able to give him some succor in the fight, but ye should have stood by him also to defend him. But now the giving of treasure shall cease for ye and ye will be shamed and will lose your land-right when the nobles learn of your inglorious deed. Death is better for every earl than ignominious life."

After this Wiglaf summoned the other earls and told them of all that had happened and of the mound that Beowulf wished them to build. Then they gathered together at the mouth of the cave and gazed with tears upon their lifeless lord and looked with awe upon the huge dragon as it lay stiff in death beside its conqueror. Afterwards, led by Wiglaf, seven chosen earls entered the cave and brought forth all the treasure, while others busied themselves in preparing the funeral pyre.

When all was ready and the huge pile of wood had been hung with helmets, war-shields and bright coats of mail, as befitted the funeral pyre of a noble warrior, the earls brought their beloved lord's body to the spot and laid it on the wood. Then they kindled the fire and stood by mourning and uttering sorrowful chants, while the smoke rose up and the fire roared and the body was consumed away. Afterwards they built a mound on the hill, making it high and broad so that it could be seen from very far away. Ten days they spent in building it; and because they desired to pay the highest of honors to Beowulf, they buried in it the whole of the treasure that the dragon had guarded, for no price was too heavy to pay as a token of their love for their lord. So the treasure even now remains in the earth, as useless as it was before.

When at last the mound was completed, the noble warriors gathered together and rode around it, lamenting their king and singing the praise of his valor and mighty deeds.

Thus mourned the people of the Geats for the fall of Beowulf, who of all kings in the world was the mildest and kindest, the most gracious to his people, and the most eager to win their praise.

The Great Knight Siegfried

Once upon a time there lived in the Netherlands, in Xante, a wonderful castle on the river Rhine, a mighty king and queen. Siegmund and Sieglinde were their names, and far and wide were they known. Yet their son, the glorious hero Siegfried, was still more widely celebrated. Even as a boy he performed so many daring feats that his bravery was talked of in all German lands.

The two most remarkable of these feats were the slaying of a frightful monster known as the "Dragon of the Linden-tree" and the capture of the rich treasure of the Nibelungs. The hoard was an ancient one and had this wonderful property—that no matter how much was taken from it the quantity was never less.

All this happened before Siegfried reached the age of manhood. When it was time for the youth to be knighted, King Siegmund sent invitations far and wide throughout the country, and a great celebration took place. Siegfried was solemnly girded with a sword and permitted to take his place among the warriors of the kingdom. Then there was a great tournament, a wonderful occasion for Siegfried, who came off victor in every encounter, although many tried warriors matched their skill against his. Altogether the festivities lasted seven whole days.

After the guests had departed, Siegfried asked permission of his parents to travel into Burgundy to seek as bride for himself Kriemhild, the maiden of whose great beauty and loveliness he had heard.

Gunther, the king of Burgundy, recognizing the young hero, went out to meet him and politely inquired the cause of his visit. Imagine his dismay when Siegfried proposed a single combat, in which the victor might claim the land and allegiance of the vanquished. Neither Gunther nor any of his knights would accept the challenge; but Gunther and his brother hastened forward with proffers of unbounded hospitality.

Siegfried lingered a year in Gunther's palace, and though he never caught a glimpse of the fair maid Kriemhild, she often admired his strength and manly beauty from behind the palace windows.

One day a herald arrived from King Ludeger of Saxony and King Ludegast of Denmark, announcing an invasion. Gunther was dismayed; but the brave Siegfried came to the rescue, saying that if Gunther would give him only one thousand brave men he would repel the enemy. This was done and the little army marched into Saxony and routed the twenty thousand valiant soldiers of the enemy's force. All the men did brave work, but Siegfried was the bravest of them all.

When the hero returned, a great celebration was held in his honor, and Kriemhild, Ute and all the ladies of the court were invited to be present at the tournament. It was there that Siegfried first saw the fair maiden. Her beauty was more wonderful than he had ever been able to imagine. What was his delight, then, to learn that he had been appointed her escort.

On the way to the tournament Kriemhild murmured her thanks for the good work Siegfried had done for her, and Siegfried vowed that he would always serve her brothers because of his great love for her.

Soon after the tournament Gunther announced his intention of winning for his wife, Brunhild, the princess of Issland, who had vowed to marry no man but the one who could surpass her in jumping, throwing a stone and casting a spear. Gunther proposed that Siegfried go with him, promising him, in return for his services, the hand of Kriemhild. Such an offer was not to be despised, and Siegfried immediately consented, advising Gunther to take only Hagen and Dankwart with him.

Gunther and the three knights set out in a small vessel. Siegfried bade his companions represent him as Gunther's vassal only; but Brunhild, seeing his giant figure and guessing its strength, imagined that he had come to woo her. She was dismayed, therefore, when she heard that he had held the stirrup for Gunther to dismount. When he entered her hall, she advanced to meet him; but he drew aside, saying that honor was due to his master Gunther.

Brunhild ordered preparations for the evening contest, and Gunther, Hagen and Dankwart trembled when they saw four men staggering under the weight of Brunhild's shield and three more staggering under the weight of her spear. Siegfried, meantime, had donned his magic cloud cloak and bade Gunther rely upon his aid.

The combat opened. Brunhild poised her spear and flung it with such force that both heroes staggered; but before she could cry out her victory Siegfried had caught the spear and flung it back with such violence that the princess fell and was obliged to acknowledge defeat.

Undaunted, she caught up a huge stone, flung it far into the distance, and then leaping, alighted beside it. No sooner had she done this than Siegfried seized the stone, flung it still farther, and lifting Gunther by his broad girdle bounded through the air with him and alighted beyond the stone. Then Brunhild knew that she had found her master.

"Come hither all my kinsmen and followers," she said, "and acknowledge my superior. I am no longer your mistress. Gunther is your lord."

The wedding was fitly celebrated and then Gunther and his bride were escorted back to Issland by a thousand Nibelung warriors whom Siegfried had gathered for the purpose. A great banquet was given upon their return, at which the impatient Siegfried ventured to remind Gunther of his promise. Brunhild protested that Gunther should not give his only sister to a menial, but Gunther gave his consent and the marriage took place immediately. The two bridal couples then sat side by side. Kriemhild's face was very happy; Brunhild's was dark and frowning.

You see, Brunhild was not pleased with the husband she had gained and preferred Siegfried. Alone with her husband the first night she bound him with her girdle and suspended him from a corner of her apartment. There she let him hang till morning. Released, Gunther sought out Siegfried and told him of the disgraceful affair.

The following evening Siegfried again donned his cloud cloak and entered the apartments of Gunther and Brunhild. As he entered he blew out the lights, caught Brunhild's hands and wrestled with her until she pleaded for mercy.

"Great king, forbear," she said. "I will henceforth be thy dutiful wife. I will do nothing to anger thee. Thou art my lord and master."

Having accomplished his purpose, Siegfried left the room, but first he took Brunhild's girdle and her ring. These he carried with him when after the festivities he and Kriemhild returned to Xante on the Rhine.

Siegmund and Sieglinde abdicated in favor of their son, and for ten years Siegfried and Kriemhild reigned happily. Then they were invited to pay a visit to Gunther and Brunhild. They accepted, leaving their little son Gunther in the care of the Nibelungs.

Brunhild received Kriemhild graciously, but at heart she was jealous and wanted Kriemhild to acknowledge her as superior. One day they had a hot dispute, Kriemhild declaring that her husband was without peer in the world, and Brunhild retorting that since he was Gunther's vassal he must be his inferior. Kriemhild made an angry avowal that she would publicly assert her rank.

Both queens parted in a rage and proceeded to attire themselves in the most gorgeous costumes they possessed. Accompanied by their ladies-in-waiting they met at the church door. Brunhild bade Kriemhild stand aside while she entered, and Kriemhild would not. A storm of words followed. Finally Kriemhild insulted the other queen by declaring that Brunhild was not a faithful wife.

"You loved Siegfried better than Gunther," she declared. "Here are your girdle and ring which my husband gave to me." So saying, she displayed the girdle and ring which Siegfried had unwisely given her when he confided to her the story of Gunther's wooing.

Brunhild summoned Gunther to defend her, and he sent for Siegfried. The latter publicly swore that his wife had not told the truth and that Brunhild had never loved him or he her.

"This quarrel is disgraceful," he said. "I will teach my wife better manners for the future." Gunther promised to do likewise.

The guests departed, but Brunhild still smarted from the insult and longed for revenge. Hagen, finding her in tears, undertook to avenge her. He continually reminded Gunther of the insult his wife had received. The king at first paid no attention to the insinuations, but at last he consented to an assault on Siegfried.

He asked the great hero to help him in a war which he pretended his old enemy Ludeger was about to bring upon him. Siegfried consented, and Kriemhild, because she loved her husband very deeply, was much troubled. In her distress she confided to Hagen that Siegfried was invulnerable except in one spot, between the shoulder blades, where a lime leaf had rested and the dragon's blood had not touched him.

"Never fear," said Hagen, "I myself will help to protect him. You sew a tiny cross on Siegfried's doublet, just over the vulnerable spot, that I may be the better able to shield him."

Kriemhild promised to obey his instructions, and Hagen departed, well pleased, to carry the news to Gunther.

At last the day came for Siegfried to leave his queen. He talked to her and comforted her and kissed her rosy lips.

"Dear heart," he said, "why all these tears? I shall not be gone long."

But she was thinking of what she had told Hagen, and wept and wept and would not be comforted.

When Siegfried joined Gunther's party he was surprised to learn that the rebellion had been quelled and that he was invited to join in a hunt instead of a fray.

So he joined the hunting party. Now Siegfried was as great a hunter as he was a warrior, and while the noonday meal was being prepared he scoured the forest, slew several wild boars, caught a bear alive and in a spirit of mischief turned him loose among the guests. Then, tired and thirsty, he sat down, calling for a drink.

Not a bit of wine was at hand; it had all been carried to another part of the forest. Hagen pointed out a spring near by and Siegfried proposed a race, offering to run in full armor while the others ran without armor or weapons. In spite of the handicap, Siegfried reached the spring first.

Always polite, Siegfried bade his host, Gunther, drink first, while he himself disarmed. Siegfried then stooped over the spring to drink, and as he stooped, Hagen, gliding behind him, drove his spear into his body at the exact spot where Kriemhild had embroidered the fatal mark.

Siegfried struggled to avenge himself, but found nothing but his shield within reach. This he flung with such force at his murderer that it knocked him down. Exhausted by the effort, the hero fell back upon the grass, cursing the treachery of Gunther and Hagen.

Curses soon gave way to thoughts of Kriemhild, however, and overcoming his anger he recommended her to the care of her brother Gunther. Then the great hero died.

The hunting party agreed to carry the body back to Worms and say that they had found it in the forest. But Hagen, bolder than the rest, ordered the bearers to deposit the corpse at Kriemhild's door, where she would see it when she went out for early mass the next morning. As he expected, Kriemhild discovered her dead lord and fell senseless upon him. Recovering, she cried out that he had been murdered: no foeman in a fair fight could have killed the glorious knight.

A great funeral took place and Siegfried's body was laid in state in the cathedral at Worms. Thither many came to view it and to express their sympathy for the widow Kriemhild. The latter, suspecting treachery, refused to listen to Gunther until he promised that all of those present at the hunt should touch the body.

"Blood will flow afresh at the murderer's touch," he said.

One by one the hunters advanced, and when Hagen touched the great warrior's form, lo, the blood flowed again from his wounds. At this the Nibelung warriors wanted to avenge the dead, but Kriemhild would not permit them to interrupt the funeral. So the ceremonies were concluded and Siegfried's body was laid to rest.

Lohengrin And Elsa The Beautiful

The young Duchess of Brabant, Elsa the Beautiful, had gone into the woods hunting, and becoming separated from her attendants, sat down to rest under a wide-branching linden-tree.

She was sorely troubled, for many lords and princes were asking for her hand in marriage. More urgent than all the others was the invincible hero, Count Telramund, her former guardian, who since the death of her father had ruled over the land with masterly hand. Now the duke, her father, on his death-bed had promised Telramund that he might have Elsa for wife, should she be willing; and Telramund was continually reminding her of this. But Elsa blushed with shame at the mere thought of such a union, for Telramund was a rough warrior, as much hated for his cruelty as he was feared for his strength. To make matters worse he was now at the court of the chosen King Henry of Saxony, threatening her with war and even worse calamities.

In the shade of the linden Elsa thought of all this, and pitied her own loneliness in that no brother or friend stood at her side to help her. Then the sweet singing of birds seemed to comfort her, and she dropped into a gentle sleep. As she dreamed it seemed to her that a young knight stepped out of the depths of the forest. Holding up a small silver bell, he spoke in friendly tones:

"If you should need my help, just ring this."

Elsa tried to take the trinket, but she could neither rise nor reach the outstretched hand. Then she awoke.

Thinking over the apparition Elsa noted a falcon circling over her head. It came nearer and finally settled on her shoulder. Around his neck hung a bell exactly like that she had seen in the dream. She loosened it, and as she did so the bird rose and flew away. But she still held the little bell in her hand, and in her soul was fresh hope and peace.

When she returned to the castle she found there a message, bidding her appear before the king in Cologne on the Rhine. Filled with confidence in the protection of higher powers, she did not hesitate to obey. In gorgeous costume, with many followers, she set out.

King Henry was a man who loved justice and exercised it, but his kingdom was in constant danger from inroads by wild Huns, and for this reason he wished to do whatever would win the favor of the powerful Count Telramund. When, however, he saw Elsa in all her beauty and innocence he hesitated in his purpose.

The plaintiff brought forward three men who testified that the duchess had entered into a secret union with one of her vassals. Only two of these men were shown to be perfidious; the testimony of the other seemed valid, though this was not enough to condemn her.

Then Telramund seized his sword, crying out that God Himself should be the judge, and that a duel should decide the matter. So a duel was arranged to take place three days later.

Elsa cast her eyes around the circle of nobles, but saw no one grasp his sword in defense of her innocence. Fear of the mighty warrior Telramund filled them all.

Remembering the little bell, she drew it forth from her pocket and rang it. The clear tones broke the stillness, grew louder and louder until they reached even the distant mountains.

"My champion will appear in the contest," she said; whereupon the count let forth such a mocking laugh that the hearts of all were filled with intense fear.

The day of the contest was at hand. The king sat on his high throne and watched the majestic river that sent its mighty waters through the valley. Princes and brave knights were gathered together. Before them stood Telramund, clad in armor, and at his side the accused Elsa, adorned with every grace that Nature can bestow.

Three times the mighty hero challenged some one to come forward as a champion for the accused girl, but no one stirred. Then arose from the Rhine the sound of sweet music; something silvery gleamed in the distance, and as it came nearer it was plain that it was a swan with silver feathers. With a silver chain he was pulling a small ship, in which lay sleeping a knight clad in bright armor.

When the bark landed, the knight awoke, rose, and blew three times on a golden horn. This was the signal that he took up the challenge. Quickly he strode into the lists.

"Your name and descent?" cried the herald.

"My name is Lohengrin," answered the stranger, "my origin royal: more it is not necessary to tell."

"Enough," broke in the king, "nobility is written on your brow."

Trumpets gave the signal for the fight to begin. Telramund's strokes fell thick as hail, but suddenly the stranger knight rose and with one fearful stroke split the count's helmet and cut his head.

"God has decided," cried the king. "His judgment is right; but you, noble knight, will help us in the campaign against the barbarian hordes and will be the leader of the detachment which the fair duchess will send from Brabant."

Gladly Lohengrin consented, and amid cries of delight from the assembled people he rode over to Elsa, who greeted him as her deliverer.

Lohengrin escorted Elsa back to Brabant, and on the way love awoke in their hearts, and they knew that they were destined for each other. In the castle of Antwerp they were pledged, and a few weeks later the marriage took place. As the bridal couple were leaving the cathedral, Lohengrin said to Elsa:

"One thing I must ask of you, and that is that you never inquire concerning my origin, for in the hour that you put that question must I surely part from you."

It was not long after the ceremony that the cry to arms came from King Henry, and Elsa accompanied her husband and his troops to Cologne, where all the counts of the kingdom were assembled. Here there were many inquiries concerning Lohengrin, and when none seemed to know of his origin, some jealously claimed that he was the son of a heathen magician, and that he gained his victories by the power of black arts.

Elsa, who had heard rumors of these charges, was deeply grieved; for she knew the noble heart of her husband. He had even relieved her fears for his safety by the assurance that he was under the protection of powers higher than human.

But she could not banish the evil rumors from her mind, and forgetting the warning her husband had given her on the day of her marriage, she dropped to her knees and asked him concerning his birth.

"Dear wife," he cried in great distress, "now will I tell to you and to the king and to all the assembled princes, what up to this time I have kept secret; but know that the time of our parting is at hand."

Then the hero led his trembling wife before the king and his nobles who were assembled on the banks of the Rhine.

"The son of Parsifal am I," he said, "the son of Parsifal, the keeper of the Holy Grail. Gladly would I have helped you, O King, in your fight against the barbarians, but an unavoidable fate calls me away. You will, however, be victorious, and under your descendants will Germany become a powerful nation."

When he finished speaking there was a deep silence, and then, as upon his arrival, there rose the sound of music—not joyful this time, but solemn, like a chant at the grave of the dead. It came nearer and again the swan and the boat appeared.

"Farewell, dear one," Lohengrin cried, folding his wife in his arms. "Too dearly did I hold you and your pleasant land of earth; now a higher duty calls me."

Weeping, Elsa clung to him; but the swan song sounded louder, like a warning. He tore himself free and stepped into the boat. Was it the ship of death and destruction, or only the ship that carried the blessed to the sacred place of the Grail? No one knew.

Elsa, lonely and sad, did not live long after the separation. Her only hope was that she would be reunited to her dear husband; and she parted willingly with her own life, as other children of earth have done when they have lost all that they held most precious.

Frithiof The Bold

Frithiof was a Norwegian hero, grandson of Viking, who was the largest and strongest man of his time. Viking had sailed the sea in a dragon ship, meeting with many adventures, and Thorsten, Frithiof's father, had likewise sailed abroad, capturing many priceless treasures and making a great name for himself.

Frithiof was entrusted to the care of Hilding, his foster father, and in his care, also, were Halfdan and Helgé, King Bélé's sons, and, some years later, their little sister, Ingeborg. Frithiof and Ingeborg became firm friends, and as the lad increased in bravery and strength, the girl increased in beauty and loveliness of soul. Hilding, noticing how each day they became fonder of each other, called Frithiof to him and bade him remember that he was only a humble subject and could never hope to wed Ingeborg, the king's only daughter, descended from the great god Odin. The warning, however, came too late, for Frithiof already loved the fair maiden, and vowed that he would have her for his bride at any cost.

Soon after this the king died, leaving his kingdom to his two sons and giving instructions that his funeral mound should be erected in sight of that of his dear friend Thorsten, so that their spirits might not be separated even in death. Then Ingeborg went to live with her brothers, the Kings of Sogn, while Frithiof retired to his own home at Framnas, closed in by the mountains and the sea.

Frithiof was now one of the wealthiest and most envied of land-owners. His treasures were richer by far than those of any king.

In the spring he held a great celebration, which the kings of Sogn and their sister Ingeborg, among many other guests, attended. Frithiof and Ingeborg were much together, and Frithiof was very happy to learn that Ingeborg returned his affection.

Great was his grief when the time came for her to sail away. Not long had she been gone, however, when he vowed to Björn, his chief companion, that he would follow after her and ask for her hand. His ship was prepared and soon he touched the shore near the temple of the god Balder.

His request was not granted and Helgé dismissed him contemptuously. In a rage at the insult Frithiof lifted his sword; but remembering that he stood on consecrated ground near Bélé's tomb, he spared the king, only cutting his heavy shield in two to show the strength of his blade.

Soon after his departure another suitor, the aged King Ring of Norway sought the hand of Ingeborg in marriage, and being refused, collected an army and prepared to make war on Helgé and Halfdan.

Then the two brothers were glad to send a messenger after Frithiof, asking his aid. The hero, still angry, refused; but he hastened at once to Ingeborg. He found her in tears at the shrine of Balder, and although it was considered a sin for a man and woman to exchange words in the sacred temple, he spoke to her, again making known his love.

The kings, her brothers, were away at war, but Frithiof stayed near Ingeborg, and when they returned, promised to free them from the oppression of Sigurd Ring if in return they would promise him the hand of their sister. But the kings had heard of how Frithiof had spoken to Ingeborg in the temple, and although they feared Sigurd they would not grant the request.

Instead he was condemned in punishment to sail away to the Orkney Islands to claim tribute from the king Angantyr.

Frithiof departed in his ship Ellida, and Ingeborg stayed behind, weeping bitterly. And as soon as the vessel was out of sight the brothers sent for two witches—Heid and Ham—bidding them stir up such a tempest on the sea that even the god-given ship Ellida could not withstand its fury.

But no tempest could frighten the brave Frithiof. Singing a cheery song he stood at the helm, caring nothing for the waves that raged about the ship. He comforted his crew, and then climbed the mast to keep a sharp lookout for danger.

From there he spied a huge whale, upon which the two witches were seated, delighted at the tempest they had stirred up. Speaking to his good ship, which could both hear and obey, he bade it run down the whale and the witches.

This Ellida did. Whale and witches sank; the sea grew red with their blood; the waves were calmed. Again the sun smiled over the hardy sailors. But many of the crew were worn out by the battle with the elements and had to be carried ashore by Frithiof and Björn when they reached the Orkney Islands.

Now the watchman at Angantyr's castle had reported the ship and the gale, and Angantyr had declared that only Frithiof and Ellida could weather such a storm. One of his vassals, Atlé, caught up his weapons and hurried forth to challenge the great hero.

Frithiof had no weapons, but with a turn of his wrist he threw his opponent.

"Go and get your weapons," Atlé said, when he saw that Frithiof would have killed him.

Knowing that Atlé was a true soldier and would not run away, Frithiof left him in search of his sword; but when he returned and found his opponent calmly awaiting death, he was generous, and bade him rise and live.

Angantyr vowed that he owed no tribute to Helgé, and would pay him none, but to Frithiof he gave a vast treasure, telling him that he might dispose of it as he would.

So Frithiof sailed back to the kings of Sogn, confident that he could win Ingeborg. What was his dismay, therefore, to learn that Helgé and Halfdan had already given their sister in marriage to Sigurd Ring. In a rage he bade his men destroy all the vessels in the harbor, while he strode toward the temple of Balder where Helgé and his wife were. He flung Angantyr's purse of gold in Helgé's face, and seeing the ring he had given to Ingeborg on the hand of Helgé's wife snatched it roughly from her. In trying to get it back she dropped the image of the god, which she had just been anointing, into the fire. It was quickly consumed, while the rising flames set fire to the temple.

Horror-stricken, Frithiof tried to stop the blaze, and when he could not, hurried away to his ship.

So Frithiof became an exile, and a wanderer on the face of the earth. For many years he lived the life of a pirate or viking, exacting tribute from other ships or sacking them if they would not pay tribute; for this occupation in the days of Frithiof was considered wholly respectable. It was followed again and again by the brave men of the North.

But Frithiof was often homesick, and longed to enter a harbor, and lead again a life of peace.

At last he decided to visit the court of Sigurd Ring and find out whether Ingeborg was really happy. Landing, he wrapped himself in an old cloak and approached the court. He found a seat on a bench near the door, as beggars usually did; but when one insulting courtier mocked him he lifted the offender in his mighty hand and swung him high over his head.

At this Sigurd Ring invited the old man to remove his mantle and take a seat near him. With surprise Sigurd and his courtiers saw step from the tattered mantle a handsome warrior, richly clad; but only Ingeborg knew who he was.

"Who are you who comes to us thus?" asked Sigurd Ring.

"I am Thiolf, a thief," was the answer, "and I have grown to manhood in the Land of Sorrow."

Sigurd invited him to remain, and he soon became the almost constant companion of the king and queen.

One spring day Sigurd and Frithiof had ridden away on a hunting expedition, and the old king being tired from the chase lay down on the ground to rest, feigning sleep. The birds and beasts of the forest drew near and whispered to Frithiof that he should slay the king and have Ingeborg for his own wife. But Frithiof was too fine and loyal to listen to such suggestions.

Awaking, Sigurd Ring called Frithiof to him.

"You are Frithiof the Bold," he said, "and from the first I knew you. Be patient now a little longer and you shall have Ingeborg, for my end is near."

Soon after this Sigurd died, commending his wife to the young hero's loving care. And at his own request the funeral feast was closed by the public betrothal of Ingeborg and Frithiof.

The people, admiring his bravery, wanted to make Frithiof king, but he would not listen to their pleadings. Instead he lifted the little son of Sigurd upon his shield.

"Behold your king," he cried, "and until he is grown to manhood I will stand beside him."

So Frithiof married his beloved Ingeborg, and later, so the story runs, he returned to his own country and built again the temple of Balder, more beautiful by far than any before.

Wayland The Smith

King Nidung had one daughter and three sons. The oldest son, Otvin, was away from court, guarding the outposts of the country; the other two sons were still children.

One day the two boys came with their bows to the great smith Wayland, asking him to make arrows for them.

"Not today," the smith answered. "I have not time; and besides, even though you are the sons of the king, I may not work for you without the wish and consent of your father. If he is willing, you may come again; but you must promise to do exactly as I tell you."

"What is that?" one of the boys ventured.

"You must," said Wayland, "come on a day when snow has freshly fallen, and you must walk facing backward all the way."

The children cared little whether they walked backward or forward, as long as they got their arrows, and so they promised. To their delight next morning they found that snow had fallen. Quickly they set out for the smithy, walking backward all the way.

"O Wayland, make us the arrows," they cried. "The king, our father, has said that we might have them."

But Wayland had no intention of making the arrows, for the king had treated him unjustly and cruelly, and he saw the opportunity for revenge. With his mighty hammer he struck the two children on the head and killed them. Then he threw their bodies into a cave adjoining the smithy.

When the children did not return the castle messengers were sent out to find them. They inquired at the smithy.

"The boys have gone," said Wayland. "I made arrows for them, and no doubt they have gone into the woods to shoot birds."

Returning to the castle the messengers saw the footprints in the snow, and since they pointed toward home, decided that the children must have gone back. But they were not there. Then Nidung sent his servants far and wide throughout the country, and when the boys were nowhere to be found, he concluded that they must have been devoured by wild animals.

When all the searches were over, Wayland brought forth the bodies of the two children, stripped the bones of flesh, whitened them, and made them into goblets and vessels for the king's table, mounting them with silver and gold. The king was delighted with them, and had them placed upon his board whenever there were guests of honor present.

A long time later, Badhild, the king's daughter, while playing with her companions in the garden one day, broke a costly ring that Nidung had given her. She was greatly vexed and feared to tell her father.

"Why not take it to Wayland to mend?" suggested one of her trusted maidens.

So Badhild gave the trinket to the girl and bade her take it to Wayland. She brought it back with her.

"Without the command of the king he will not mend it," she said, "unless the king's daughter herself will come to him."

Badhild set out immediately for the smithy. There Wayland substituted for her ring his own, which had the curious magic power of making its wearer fall in love with the smith.

The smith slipped the jewel on her finger, gazed into her eyes and said, "This ring you shall keep as well as your own, if you will be my bride."

The maiden could not refuse, and so the two were married, agreeing to keep their union a secret.

About this time Eigil, the brother of Wayland, came to the court of Nidung. He was a celebrated man and the most skilful master of the bow to be found anywhere in the world. The king welcomed him, and he remained a long time at the court. One day Nidung proposed that, since he was such a skilful bowman, he should try shooting an apple from the head of his own son. Eigil agreed.

"You may have only one trial," the king said.

So an apple was placed on the head of Eigil's three-year-old son, and Eigil, taking his bow, aimed, and with the first arrow struck the apple in the center, so that it fell from the child's head.

"Why did you have three arrows?" the king asked.

"Sire," replied Eigil, "I will not lie to you. If I had pierced my son with the first arrow, the other two would have pierced you."

The king, strange to say, did not take offense at this speech, but on the contrary showed Eigil still greater favor than he had in the past.

The archer frequently visited his brother Wayland, but Badhild came but seldom to her husband's house. One day the two came together at Wayland's special request. When they were leaving Wayland embraced Badhild and said to her:

"You will be the mother of a boy—your child and mine. It may be that I shall go away from here and never see his face; but you must tell him that I have made for him worthy weapons and stowed them in safety in the place where the water enters and the wind goes out (the forge)."

The next time Wayland saw Eigil he bade him bring to him all kinds of feathers, large and small.

"I wish to make for myself a doublet of feathers," he explained.

Then Eigil shot many birds of prey and brought their feathers to Wayland. From them he made a flying shirt, clad in which he looked more like an eagle than a man.

Eigil admired the workmanship and Wayland asked him to try it.

"How shall I rise, how fly, and how alight?" asked Eigil.

"You must rise against the wind, and fly first low and then high, but you must alight with the wind."

Eigil did as he was told, and had a good deal of trouble in alighting. Finally he knocked his head with such force on the ground that he lost consciousness. When he came to himself Wayland spoke:

"Tell me, brother Eigil, do you like the shirt?"

"If it were as easy to alight as it is to fly," was the answer, "I should fly away and you would never see me again."

"I will alter what is wrong," said the smith, making a slight change in the shirt. Then with Eigil's help he put on the feathers, flapped his wings and rose into the air. He lighted on a turret of the castle and called down to Eigil.

"I did not tell you the truth when I said that you should alight with the wind, for I knew that if you found out how easy it was to fly you would never give me the shirt back again. You can see for yourself that all birds rise against the wind and alight in the same way. I am going home to my own country, but first I must have a few words with Nidung. And, remember, if he bids you shoot me, shoot under the left wing, for there I have fastened a bladder filled with blood."

With these words Wayland flew to the highest tower of the king's castle and called to the king as he passed with his courtiers.

"Are you a bird, Wayland?" asked the king.

"Sometimes I am a bird and sometimes a man," was the reply; "but now I am going away from here and never again will you have me in your power. Listen while I speak. You promised once to give me your daughter and the half of your kingdom, but you made of me instead an outcast—because I defended myself and killed the wretches who would have taken my life.

"You surprised me while I slept and stole my arms and my treasures; and not satisfied with that you laid a net for my feet and made of me a cripple. But I have had my revenge. Do you know where your sons are?"

"My sons!" cried Nidung. "Oh, tell me what you know of them."

"I will tell you, but first you must swear to me by the deck of the ship and the edge of the shield, by the back of the horse and the blade of the sword that you will do no harm to my wife and child."

Nidung swore and Wayland began his speech:

"Go to my smithy, and there in the cave you will find the remains of your sons. I killed them, and of their bones made vessels for your table. Your daughter Badhild is my wife. So have I repaid evil with evil, and our connection is ended."

With these words he flew away, while Nidung in great anger cried: "Eigil, shoot at Wayland."

"I cannot harm my own brother," replied Eigil.

"Shoot," cried the king, "or I will kill you."

Then Eigil laid an arrow in his bow and shot Wayland as he had been instructed, under his left arm, until the blood flowed and everyone thought that the great smith had received his death wound.

But Wayland, unharmed, flew away to Zealand and made his home there in his father's land.

Nidung, meantime, was sad and unhappy, and it was not long before he died and Otvin, his son, succeeded to the throne.

Otvin was soon loved and honored throughout the kingdom because of his great justice and kindness. His sister lived with him at court, and there her son, Widge, was born.

One day Wayland sent messengers to Otvin, asking for peace and pardon, and when these were granted he traveled again to Jutland and was received with great honor.

The mighty smith was very glad to see his wife again and very proud of his three-year-old son; but he would not yield to

Otvin's request that he remain in Jutland. Instead he returned to Zealand with Badhild and Widge, and there they lived happily for many years.

Wayland was known throughout all the world for his knowledge and skill, and his son Widge was a powerful hero, whose praises were much celebrated in song.

So ends the story of Wayland, the great smith of the northern countries.

Twardowski, The Polish Faust

Toward the close of the eighteenth century there was pointed out to visitors in the old town of Krakau the house of the magician Twardowski, who quite properly was called the Faust of Poland, because of his dealings with the Evil One.

In his youth Twardowski had followed the study of medicine, and with such industry, such eagerness and such a clear mind did he practice his profession that it was not long before he was the most celebrated doctor in all Poland. But Twardowski was not satisfied with this. He craved greater and still greater power.

At last one day, as he was reading, he found in an old book of magic that for which he had long been seeking — the formula for summoning the devil. When night came a storm had risen, but caring not for that he hurried away to the lonely mountain Kremenki. There, in a rudely constructed hut, he began his incantations.

Before long there was an earthquake; great rocks were loosened, the ground opened at Twardowski's feet and flames leaped out; and in the flames appeared the Evil One himself, in the form of a man, clad in a red cloak with the well-known pointed red cap.

"What do you wish?" the devil asked.

"The power of your most secret wisdom," was the answer.

"And how is this to be done?"

"You shall make me the most celebrated of all the learned men of the century, and shall besides give me such happiness as no man has ever enjoyed upon this earth before."

"So be it," said the devil. "But on condition that at the end of seven years I gain possession of your soul."

"You may take me," answered Twardowski, "but only in Rome may you have power over me. Thither, at the end of seven years, will I go."

The devil hesitated over this clause, but thinking of the fun he could have in the holy city, finally agreed. Leaning against the wall of stone he wrote the compact, which Twardowski, making a slight wound in his arm, signed with his own blood.

When Twardowski descended from the mountain and made his way, book under arm, through the valley, he heard the bells in all the towers of the city ringing out clearly and solemnly on the still night air. He listened, wondering at the unaccustomed noise, then hurried into the town, inquiring from every one he met what the occasion was. But no one seemed to have heard the sound.

Then a deep feeling of sadness came over him as he realized the meaning of the bells. They were the funeral knell of his own soul.

When morning came, however, doubts were forgotten, and Twardowski was glad to have the devil at his command. The first thing that he demanded was to have all the silver of Poland gathered together in one place and covered over with great mounds of sand.

Similar requests followed, and it was not long before the devil repented of his bargain. One day it would please Twardowski to fly without wings through the air; on another, to the delight of the crowd, to gallop backward on a cock; on another to float in a boat without a rudder or sail, accompanied by some maiden who for the moment had inflamed his heart. One day, by the use of his magic mirror, he set fire to the castle of an enemy a mile away. This last feat made him greatly feared by people far and wide.

At last the seven years were up. The devil appeared to Twardowski and said:

"Twardowski, the time of our pact is over, and I command you to fulfill your promise and go to Rome."

"What shall I do there?"

"Give me your immortal soul," was the answer.

"Do you think I am a fool?" asked Twardowski.

"You gave me your promise to go to Rome after seven years."

"That I have already done," said Twardowski, "and I did not promise to stay in Rome."

"Noble deceiver!" exclaimed the Evil One.

"Stupid devil!" cried Twardowski.

Then after a struggle the devil vanished and Twardowski returned home.

For over a year he pored incessantly over his books of magic, until at last he found a formula for warding off death. Then he called his disciple Famulus to him and explained that he was going to test the formula.

"You have always obliged me without question," said Twardowski, "and I expect you to now. Take this knife and thrust it into my heart."

"God forbid!" cried Famulus.

"Why are you frightened? I know what I am doing. Take the knife and kill me, as the parchment directs."

"I cannot."

"You must," insisted Twardowski.

"It is impossible!"

"No more exclamations. Do as I tell you."

"Oh, oh, oh!" wailed Famulus.

"Strike!" thundered Twardowski, "or I will kill you this instant."

Then Famulus did as he was bid and forced the blade into his master's heart.

Twardowski uttered a low cry, fell, and was soon dead.

Famulus dropped trembling into a chair and covered his face with his hands. Then he remembered that he must read the remainder of the parchment in order to find out what he must do to restore the body to life.

Then he set about the task, severed the limbs of the dead body, and worked and brewed and distilled until the elixir described in the parchment was prepared.

With the elixir he rubbed the members of the master's body, put them together, and laid the corpse in a coffin. This he buried on the following night, explaining to Twardowski's friends that such had been the master's wish.

Now the parchment stated that the body must remain in the grave seven years, seven months, seven days and seven hours; so Famulus could do nothing but wait. At last the time had expired, and on a snowy, cold December night he found his way to the grave. He dug out the coffin, brushed off the snow and earth, opened the casket and found—not the body of Twardowski, but that of a child who lay sleeping in a bed of fragrant violets.

"The child is like Twardowski," Famulus thought, and he gathered him up under his cloak and carried him home. The next morning the child was the size of a twelve-year old; and after seven weeks he was a full-grown man.

Twardowski, who now seemed quite himself, only younger, and stronger, thanked Famulus and resumed again his study of magic. He desired, above all things, to be freed forever from his compact with the devil. This, he read in one of the books, he might do if he would brave the terrors of the underworld.

So Twardowski determined to enter the gates of hell. At his magic speech the ground opened and he began the path of descent. Blue flames lighted the way. Deeper and deeper he went through dark and winding passages. At last he reached the underworld itself, and many awful sights did he behold.

And the farther he went the more frightened did he become. He could not help feeling that the devil had plotted something against him. Finally he found himself in a small room, and cast a hasty glance around, looking for a means of escape.

Seeing a child in a cradle in one corner of the room he seized it hastily, threw his cloak around it, and was about to leave when the door opened and the Evil One entered.

He made a respectful bow and said, "Will you be good enough to go with me now?"

"Why so?" asked Twardowski, obstinately.

"Because of our agreement."

"But," said the magician, "only in Rome have you power over me."

"Yes," replied the devil, "and Rome is the name of this house."

"You think to trick me by a pun; but you cannot. I carry this talisman of innocence," and throwing aside his cloak, he disclosed the sleeping child.

Anger showed in the face of the devil; but he stepped nearer to Twardowski and said softly:

"What are you thinking of, Twardowski? Have you forgotten your promise? The nobleman's word is sacred to him."

Pride awoke in the breast of the magician.

"I must keep my word," he said, laying the child back in the crib, and surrendering himself.

On the shoulders of the devil two wings appeared, like the wings of a bat. He seized Twardowski and flew away with him, mounting higher and higher into the night. The magician was so terrified and suffered such anguish in the clutches of the Evil One that in a few moments he was changed into an old man, but he did not lose consciousness. At last so high were they that cities appeared like flies and Krakau with its mighty turrets like two spiders. Deeply moved, Twardowski looked down upon the scene of all his struggles and all his joys.

But higher and higher they went—higher than any eagle has ever flown—and more lonely and more fearful did it seem to Twardowski. Only occasionally bright stars passed by them, or fiery meteors, leaving a long streak of light behind.

At last they came to the moon, which stared at them with dead eyes. Then a song that Twardowski had read in his mother's hymn book rose to his lips. And as he repeated mechanically the prayer his mother had taught him an angel suddenly appeared and said:

"Satan, let Twardowski go; and you, Twardowski, hang you there between heaven and earth, to atone for your sin until the Last Judgment. Then will you be reunited with your mother in heaven. The prayer which you remembered in your hour of need has saved you."

And so, according to the story, Twardowski is suspended in the vault of heaven to this very day.

Ilia Muromec Of Russia

When we think of Russia we think of a great dark country—a country of long winters and abundant snow and ice. It was here, long ago, in the city of Kiev, that the hero Ilia Muromec was born.

There was at that time a great castle in the city, and this was well protected by Ilia Muromec and his twelve armed knights. For thirty long years had they kept watch at their post and no stranger had ever passed by them.

But one morning Dobrnja, the knight after Ilia Muromec most powerful, perceived on the ground the imprint of a horse's hoof. Then he said to the knights:

"Now is the mighty Zidovin in the neighborhood of our castle. What is your will?"

The knights with one accord agreed that Dobrnja should ride out against the stranger. So Dobrnja mounted his war-horse and galloped forth to meet Zidovin, calling to him in a deep, gruff voice:

"Here, my insolent sir, you have come all the way to our castle and have omitted to send greeting to our captain Ilia Muromec, or to inform him of your approach."

When Zidovin heard these words he turned quickly and rode toward Dobrnja with such force that springs and lakes appeared wherever the hoofs of his black horse touched the ground. And the trembling of the earth caused great waves to rise on the sea.

Dobrnja was so frightened that he jerked his horse about and with the swiftness of a cyclone galloped back to the castle. When he entered, almost exhausted, he told in great excitement of his encounter.

Immediately Ilia decided to go forth himself against the enemy, and all the entreaties of his knights could not restrain him. So he rode out to a high point where he could see Zidovin, watch him as he threw his hundred-weight club up into the clouds, caught it with one hand, and swung it around in the air as if it had been a feather.

Then Ilia spurred his horse and rode toward Zidovin. A horrible fight ensued. Swords clashed and deep fissures were made in the earth, but neither knight fell. It seemed as if both heroes had grown fast to their saddles, so unshakeable were they.

At last they jumped from their horses and fought hand to hand with lances. All day long and all night long they struggled, until Ilia finally fell wounded to the ground. Zidovin kneeled on his breast, drew out his sharp knife, and was about to cut off the head of his enemy.

Ilia meantime was thinking, "Surely the holy fathers did not lie to me when they said that I should not lose my life in battle."

Then suddenly he felt his strength redoubled, and he hurled Zidovin from him with such force that his body touched the clouds before it fell again in the moist earth at his feet. Cutting off the warrior's head, he mounted his horse and rode back to the castle. To his knights he said:

"Thirty years have I ridden in the field and thirty years have I fought with heroes and tested my strength; but such a mighty man as Zidovin have I in all that time never met."

Kralewitz Marko Of Servia

Kralewitz Marko was the son of a Servian king who lived many, many years ago. He was very fond of hunting, and one day he rode forth on his horse Saria to the mountain Sargau. Being tired, he dismounted, tied his horse to a tree, sat down in its shade and fell asleep.

And as he slept it happened that Arbanes Neda with his seven brothers rode by. They all dismounted, lifted Kralewitz, bound him to his horse, and rode away with him to Jedrena, where they presented him to the vizier.

Highly pleased over the gift, the vizier took the king's son and threw him into prison. Two long years Kralewitz lay there, longing for liberty and home. Then he learned that in a few days he was to be executed.

Immediately he wrote a letter to his friend, Milos Obilis, asking for help. This important message he entrusted to his only companion, a white falcon. Tying the letter under the bird's wing he set it free.

The falcon easily found its way, alighted on Milos' window, and was admitted. Scarcely had Milos read the letter, when he and two of his friends were ready to set out for Jedrena. They reached there the day before the execution.

In the morning the gate of the city was opened and Marko was led out. Milos and his companions accompanied the mournful procession to an open field in which the execution was to take place. Two Arabs stood up with gleaming swords prepared to cut off Marko's head.

"Hold on, brothers," cried Milos. "I will give you a sharper sword with which to cut off the malicious head of the noble Piam. See, with this sword did the good-for-nothing treacherously slay my father. Cursed be his hand!"

With these words he rushed to Marko's side; then with one swift stroke he cut off the head of one Arab, and with another the head of the other.

With still another stroke he severed the chains that bound Marko, and Marko, seizing a sword, swung himself into his saddle, and with his friends began to attack the horde of Turks. Frightened, the Turks fled before them, and Marko and his companions returned to their own country.

Marko waited for and soon found the opportunity of showing his gratitude to his friend, for Milos and two of his brothers were thrown into prison in Varadin. Milos wrote with his own blood a letter to Marko, asking for help.

Then the king's son sprang to his horse Saria and rode to Varadin. Outside of the city he dismounted, stuck his spear in the earth, tied Saria and began drinking the black wine which he had brought with him. He poured it into huge beakers, half of which he drank himself, and half of which he gave to Saria.

At the same time a beautiful maiden, the daughter-in-law of the general, passed by. When she saw the king's son she was frightened and ran and told her father-in-law.

Then the general sent out his son Velimir with three hundred men to take Marko prisoner. The knights encircled Kralewitz Marko, but he continued drinking his wine and paid no attention to them. But Saria noticed them, and drawing near her master began beating the ground with her hoofs.

At this Marko looked up and saw himself surrounded. He emptied his beaker, threw it to the ground, and sprang to his horse.

Like a falcon among doves Marko charged against the enemy. He cut off the heads of some and drove the rest before him into the Danube. Velimir tried to flee, but Marko threw him from his horse, tied his hands and feet and bound him to Saria. Then again he began to drink his wine.

All this the maiden watched and reported to her father. He gathered together three thousand knights and rode forth against the stranger. They surrounded Marko, but he was undismayed. Bravely he charged against them, his sword in his right hand, his spear in his left, and the reins held between his teeth.

Every knight he touched with either sword or spear fell instantly to the ground, and when Vuca, the general, wholly dismayed, tried to escape on his fiery Arabian horse, Marko followed him, threw him, bound him, and led him to the place where his son lay. Then he bound the two together, tossed them on the saddle of the Arabian horse and rode home. There he put them in prison.

Hearing this, the wife of the general wrote a letter to Marko, begging for mercy for her husband and son. Marko promised to release them on condition that she release Milos and his brothers. This she did, honoring them and making them rich presents.

"Now, for the love of Heaven," said she, "see that my husband and my son return to me."

"Never fear," answered Milos. "Give me the general's black horse; adorn him as the general adorned him; give me a golden chariot with twelve horses, such as the general rides in when he journeys to the emperor in Vienna; and give me the robe that the general wears on state occasions."

The wife provided all that he asked, and gave the prisoners for themselves a thousand ducats. Then they rode away.

Marko welcomed them, released the general and his son and provided them with a strong body-guard back to Varadin. Then Milos and his brothers divided the ducats among them, kissed the hand of the king's son, and rode away into their own country.

The Decision Of Libuscha

There dwelt once in the neighborhood of Grünberg Castle in Bohemia two brothers—Staglow and Chrudis, of the distinguished family of Klemowita—and these two had fallen into a fierce dispute over the inheritance of their father's lands. The older son Chrudis thought that he should inherit all of the estate—and that is the custom in some countries, you know—while the younger son, Staglow, declared that the property should be equally divided.

Now it happened that a sister of the princess Libuscha Vyched lived at the court. She entreated the princess to settle the quarrel according to law.

The princess yielded to her wish, and decided that the brothers should either inherit their father's estate jointly or divide it into equal shares.

All the lords of the country assembled to hear the rendering of the decision—brave knights from far and near. Chrudis and Staglow, of course, were present, very curious to hear what their princess would decide. Pungel of Hadio, proclaimed far and wide as the bravest of all the knights of Bohemia, was also among the company.

The princess herself rendered the decision, standing in white robes before her people. The two brothers stood near, and scarcely had the last word been uttered when the knight Chrudis, who, as first-born, claimed the estate for himself, sprang excitedly to his feet, mocking and insulting the princess. "Poor people," he said, addressing the assembly, "I am sorry for you who have to be ruled over by a girl."

Deeply grieved, the maiden-princess Libuscha rose, explaining that she would no longer rule alone. She commanded the people to choose her a husband.

"No matter whom you choose," she declared, "I will abide by your decision."

Thereupon the assembled subjects cried out that they would have Pungel of Hadio as prince; and Libuscha, stepping toward him, extended her hand to him in token of her agreement.

Thus did Pungel become the liege lord of the Bohemian nobles.

No one knows how long ago all this happened, for the manuscript that tells the story was very old when it was discovered in the year 1817. It had lain for many, many years among other old documents in the great chests that lined the walls of the courtroom in the ancient Castle Grünberg in Bohemia. The manuscript is now in a great museum in Prague, and perhaps, some day, when you go there, you will see it for yourself.

Count Roland Of France

The trumpets sounded and the army went on its way to France. The next day King Charles called his lords together. "You see," said he, "these narrow passes. Whom shall I place to command the rear-guard? Choose you a man yourselves."

Said Ganelon, "Whom should we choose but my son-in-law, Count Roland? You have no man in your host so valiant. Of a truth he will be the salvation of France."

The King said when he heard these words, "What ails you, Ganelon? You look like to one possessed."

When Count Roland knew what was proposed concerning him, he spake out as a true knight should speak: "I am right thankful to you, father-in-law, that you have caused me to be put in this place. Of a truth the King of France shall lose nothing by my means, neither charger, nor mule, nor pack-horse, nor beast of burden."

Then Roland turned to the King and said, "Give me twenty thousand only, so they be men of valor, and I will keep the passes in all safety. So long as I shall live, you need fear no man."

Then Roland mounted his horse. With him were Oliver, his comrade, and Otho and Berenger, and Gerard of Roussillon, an aged warrior, and others, men of renown. And Turpin the Archbishop cried, "By my head, I will go also." So they chose twenty thousand warriors with whom to keep the passes.

Meanwhile King Charles had entered the valley of Roncesvalles. High were the mountains on either side of the way, and the valleys were gloomy and dark. But when the army had passed through the valley, they saw the fair land of Gascony, and as they saw it they thought of their homes and their wives and daughters. There was not one of them but wept for very tenderness of heart. But of all that company there was none sadder than the King himself, when he thought how he had left his nephew Count Roland behind him in the passes of Spain.

And now the Saracen King Marsilas began to gather his army. He laid a strict command on all his nobles and chiefs that they should bring with them to Saragossa as many men as they could gather together. And when they were come to the city, it being the third day from the issuing of the King's command, they saluted the great image of Mahomet, the false prophet, that stood on the topmost tower. This done they went forth from the city gates. They made all haste, marching across the mountains and valleys of Spain till they came in sight of the standard of France, where Roland and Oliver and the Twelve Peers were ranged in battle array.

The Saracen champions donned their coats of mail, of double substance most of them, and they set upon their heads helmets of Saragossa of well-tempered metal, and they girded themselves with swords of Vienna. Fair were their shields to view; their lances were from Valentia; their standards were of white, blue, and red. Their mules they left with the servants, and, mounting their chargers, so moved forwards. Fair was the day and bright the sun, as their armor flashed in the light, and the drums were beaten so loudly that the Frenchmen heard the sound.

Said Oliver to Roland, "Comrade, methinks we shall soon do battle with the Saracens."

"God grant it," answered Roland. "'Tis our duty to hold the place for the King, and we will do it, come what may. As for me, I will not set an ill example."

Oliver climbed to the top of a hill, and saw from thence the whole army of the heathen. He cried to Roland his companion, "I see the flashing of arms. We men of France shall have no small trouble therefrom. This is the doing of Ganelon the traitor."

"Be silent," answered Roland, "till you shall know; say no more about him."

Oliver looked again from the hilltop, and saw how the Saracens came on. So many there were that he could not count their battalions. He descended to the plain with all speed, and came to the array of the French, and said, "I have seen more heathen than man ever yet saw together upon the earth. There are a hundred thousand at the least. We shall have such a battle with them as has never before been fought. My brethren of France, quit you like men, be strong; stand firm that you be not conquered." And all the army shouted with one voice, "Cursed be he that shall fly."

Then Oliver turned to Roland, and said, "Sound your horn; my friend, Charles will hear it, and will return."

"I were a fool," answered Roland, "so to do. Not so; but I will deal these heathen some mighty blows with Durendal, my sword. They have been ill-advised to venture into these passes. I swear that they are condemned to death, one and all."

After a while, Oliver said again, "Friend Roland, sound your horn of ivory. Then will the King return, and bring his army with him, to our help." But Roland answered again, "I will not do dishonor to my kinsmen, or to the fair land of France. I have my sword; that shall suffice for me. These evil-minded heathen are gathered together against us to their own hurt. Surely not one of them shall escape from death."

"As for me," said Oliver, "I see not where the dishonor would be. I saw the valleys and the mountains covered with the great multitude of Saracens. Theirs is, in truth, a mighty array, and we are but few."

"So much the better," answered Roland. "It makes my courage grow. 'Tis better to die than to be disgraced. And remember, the harder our blows the more the King will love us."

Roland was brave, but Oliver was wise. "Consider," he said, "comrade. These enemies are over-near to us, and the King over-far. Were he here, we should not be in danger; but there are some here today who will never fight in another battle."

Then Turpin the Archbishop struck spurs into his horse, and rode to a hilltop. Then he turned to the men of France, and spake: "Lords of France, King Charles has left us here; our King he is, and it is our duty to die for him. Today our Christian Faith is in peril: do ye fight for it. Fight ye must; be sure of that, for there under your eyes are the Saracens. Confess, therefore, your sins, and pray to God that He have mercy upon you. And now for your soul's health I will give you all absolution. If you die, you will be God's martyrs, every one of you, and your places are ready for you in His Paradise."

Thereupon the men of France dismounted, and knelt upon the ground, and the Archbishop blessed them in God's name. "But look," said he, "I set you a penance—smite these pagans." Then the men of France rose to their feet. They had received absolution, and were set free from all their sins, and the Archbishop had blessed them in the name of God. After this they mounted their swift steeds, and clad themselves in armor, and made themselves ready for the battle.

Said Roland to Oliver, "Brother, you know that it is Ganelon who has betrayed us. Good store he has had of gold and silver as a reward; 'tis the King Marsilas that has made merchandise of us, but verily it is with our swords that he shall be paid." So saying, he rode on to the pass, mounted on his good steed Veillantif. His spear he held with the point to the sky; a white flag it bore with fringes of gold which fell down to his hands. A stalwart man was he, and his countenance was fair and smiling. Behind him followed Oliver, his friend; and the men of France pointed to him, saying, "See our champion!" Pride was in his eye when he looked towards the Saracens; but to the men of

France his regard was all sweetness and humility. Full courteously he spake to them:

"Ride not so fast, my lords," he said; "verily these heathen are come hither, seeking martyrdom. 'Tis a fair spoil that we shall gather from them today. Never has King of France gained any so rich." And as he spake, the two hosts came together.

Said Oliver, "You did not deem it fit, my lord, to sound your horn. Therefore you lack the help which the King would have sent. Not his the blame, for he knows nothing of what has chanced. But do you, lords of France, charge as fiercely as you may, and yield not one whit to the enemy. Think upon these two things only—how to deal a straight blow and to take it. And let us not forget King Charles' cry of battle."

Then all the men of France with one voice cried out, "Mountjoy!" He that heard them so cry had never doubted that they were men of valor. Proud was their array as they rode on to battle, spurring their horses that they might speed the more. And the Saracens, on their part, came forward with a good heart. Thus did the Frenchmen and the heathen meet in the shock of battle.

Full many of the heathen warriors fell that day. Not one of the Twelve Peers of France but slew his man. But of all none bore himself so valiantly as Roland. Many a blow did he deal to the enemy with his mighty spear, and when the spear was shivered in his hand, fifteen warriors having fallen before it, then he seized his good sword Durendal, and smote man after man to the ground. Red was he with the blood of his enemies, red was his hauberk, red his arms, red his shoulders, aye, and the neck of his horse. Not one of the Twelve lingered in the rear, or was slow to strike, but Count Roland was the bravest of the brave. "Well done, sons of France!" cried Turpin the Archbishop, when he saw them lay on in such sort.

Next to Roland for valor and hardihood came Oliver, his companion. Many a heathen warrior did he slay, till at last his spear was shivered in his hand. "What are you doing, comrade?" cried Roland, when he was aware of the mishap. "A man wants no staff in such a battle as this. 'Tis the steel and nothing else that he must have. Where is your sword Hautclere, with its hilt of gold and its pommel of crystal?"

"On my word," said Oliver, "I have not had time to draw it; I was so busy with striking." But as he spake he drew the good sword from its scabbard, and smote a heathen knight, Justin of the Iron Valley. A mighty blow it was, cleaving the man in twain down to his saddle—aye, and the saddle itself with its adorning of gold and jewels, and the very backbone also of the steed whereon he rode, so that horse and man fell dead together on the plains. "Well done!" cried Roland; "you are a true brother of mine. 'Tis such strokes as this that make the King love us."

Nevertheless, for all the valor of Roland and his fellows the battle went hard with the men of France. Many lances were shivered, many flags torn, and many gallant youths cut off in their prime. Never more would they see mother and wife. It was an ill deed that the traitor Ganelon wrought when he sold his fellows to King Marsilas!

And now there befell a new trouble. King Almaris, with a great host of heathen, coming by an unknown way, fell upon the rear of the host where there was another pass. Fiercely did the noble Walter that kept the same charge the newcomers, but they overpowered him and his followers. He was wounded with four several lances, and four times did he swoon, so that at the last he was constrained to leave the field of battle, that he might call the Count Roland to his aid. But small was the aid which Roland could give him or any one. Valiantly he held up the battle, and with him Oliver, and Turpin the Archbishop, and others also; but the lines of the men of France were broken, and their armor thrust through and their spears shivered, and their flags trodden in the dust. For all this they made such slaughter among the heathen that King Almaris, who led the armies of the enemy, scarcely could win back his way to his own people, wounded in four places and sorely spent. A right good warrior was he; had he but been a Christian, but few had matched him in battle.

Count Roland saw how grievously his people had suffered and spake thus to Oliver his comrade: "Dear comrade, you see how many brave men lie dead upon the ground. Well may we mourn for fair France, widowed as she is of so many valiant champions. But why is our King not here? O Oliver, my brother, what shall we do to send him tidings of our state?" "I know not," answered Oliver. "Only this I know—that death is to be chosen rather than dishonor."

After a while Roland said again, "I shall blow my horn; King Charles will hear it, where he has encamped beyond the passes, and he and his host will come back."

"That would be ill done," answered Oliver, "and shame both you and your race. When I gave you this counsel you would have none of it. Now I like it not. 'Tis not for a brave man to sound the horn and cry for help now that we are in such case."

"The battle is too hard for us," said Roland again, "and I shall sound my horn, that the King may hear."

And Oliver answered again, "When I gave you this counsel, you scorned it. Now I myself like it not. 'Tis true that had the King been here, we had not suffered this loss. But the blame is not his. 'Tis your folly, Count Roland, that has done to death all these men of France. But for that we should have conquered in this battle, and have taken and slain King Marsilas. But now we can do nothing for France and the King. We can but die. Woe is me for our country, aye, and for our friendship, which will come to a grievous end this day."

The Archbishop perceived that the two friends were at variance, and spurred his horse till he came where they stood. "Listen to me," he said, "Sir Roland and Sir Oliver. I implore you not to fall out with each other in this fashion. We, sons of France, that are in this place, are of a truth condemned to death, neither will the sounding of your horn save us, for the King is far away, and cannot come in time. Nevertheless, I hold it to be well that you should sound it. When the King and his army shall come, they will find us dead—that I know full well. But they will avenge us, so that our enemies shall not go away rejoicing. And they will also recover our bodies, and will carry them away for burial in holy places, so that the dogs and wolves shall not devour them."

"You say well," cried Roland, and he put his horn to his lips, and gave so mighty a blast upon it, that the sound was heard thirty leagues away. King Charles and his men heard it, and the King said, "Our countrymen are fighting with the enemy." But Ganelon answered, "Sire, had any but you so spoken, I had said that he spoke falsely."

Then Roland blew his horn a second time; with great pain and anguish of body he blew it, and the red blood gushed from his lips; but the sound was heard yet farther than at first. Again the King heard it, and all his nobles, and all his men. "That," said he, "is Roland's horn; he never had sounded it were he not in battle with the enemy." But Ganelon answered again: "Believe me, Sire, there is no battle. You are an old man, and you have the fancies of a child. You know what a mighty man of valor is this Roland. Think you that any one would dare to attack him? No one, of a truth. Ride on, Sire; why halt you here? The fair land of France is yet far away."

Roland blew his horn a third time, and when the King heard it he said, "He that blew that horn drew a deep breath." And Duke Naymes cried out, "Roland is in trouble; on my conscience he is fighting with the enemy. Some one has betrayed him; 'tis he, I doubt not, that would deceive you now. To arms, Sire! Utter your war-cry, and help your own house and your country. You have heard the cry of the noble Roland."

Then King Charles bade all the trumpets sound, and forthwith all the men of France armed themselves, with helmets, and hauberks, and swords with pommels of gold. Mighty were their shields, and their lances strong, and the flags that they carried were white and red and blue. And when they made an end of their arming they rode back with all haste. There was not one of them but said to his comrade, "If we find Roland yet alive, what mighty strokes will we strike for him!"

But Ganelon the King handed over to the knaves of his kitchen. "Take this traitor," said he, "who has sold his country." Ill did Ganelon fare among them. They pulled out his hair and his beard and smote him with their staves; then they put a great chain, such as that with which a bear is bound, about his neck, and made him fast to a pack-horse.

This done, the King and his army hastened with all speed to the help of Roland. In the van and the rear sounded the trumpets as though they would answer Roland's horn. Full of wrath was King Charles as he rode; full of wrath were all the men of France. There was not one among them but wept and sobbed; there was not one but prayed, "Now, may God keep Roland alive till we come to the battle-field, so that we may strike a blow for him." Alas! it was all in vain; they could not come in time for all their speed.

Count Roland looked round on the mountain-sides and on the plains. Alas! how many noble sons of France he saw lying dead upon them! "Dear friends," he said, weeping as he spoke, "may God have mercy on you and receive you into His Paradise! More loyal followers have I never seen. How is the fair land of France widowed of her bravest, and I can give you no help. Oliver, dear comrade, we must not part. If the enemy slay me not here, surely I shall be slain by sorrow. Come then, let us smite these heathen."

Thus did Roland again charge the enemy, his good sword Durendal in his hand; as the stag flies before the hounds, so did the heathen fly before Roland. "By my faith," cried the Archbishop when he saw him, "that is a right good knight! Such courage, and such a steed, and such arms I love well to see. If a man be not brave and a stout fighter, he had better by far be a monk in some cloister where he may pray all day long for our sins."

Now the heathen, when they saw how few the Frenchmen were, took fresh courage. And the Caliph, spurring his horse, rode against Oliver and smote him in the middle of his back, making his spear pass right through him. "That is a shrewd blow," he cried; "I have avenged my friends and countrymen upon you."

Then Oliver knew he was stricken to death, but he would not fall unavenged. With his great sword Hautclere he smote the Caliph on his head and cleft it to the teeth. "Curse on you, pagan. Neither your wife nor any woman in the land of your birth shall boast that you have taken a penny's worth from King Charles!" But to Roland he cried, "Come, comrade, help me; well I know that we two shall part in great sorrow this day."

Roland came with all speed, and saw his friend, how he lay all pale and fainting on the ground and how the blood gushed in great streams from his wound. "I know not what to do," he cried. "This is an ill chance that has befallen you. Truly France is bereaved of her bravest son." So saying he went near to swoon in the saddle as he sat. Then there befell a strange thing. Oliver had lost so much of his blood that he could not any more see clearly or know who it was that was near him. So he raised up his arm and smote with all his strength that yet remained to him on the helmet of Roland his friend. The helmet he cleft in twain to the visor; but by good fortune it wounded not the head.

Roland looked at him and said in a gentle voice, "Did you this of set purpose? I am Roland your friend, and have not harmed you."

"Ah!" said Oliver, "I hear you speak, but I cannot see you. Pardon me that I struck you; it was not done of set purpose."

"It harmed me not," answered Roland; "with all my heart and before God I forgive you." And this was the way these two friends parted at the last.

And now Oliver felt the pains of death come over him. He could no longer see nor hear. Therefore he turned his thoughts to making his peace with God, and clasping his hands lifted them to heaven and made his confession. "O Lord," he said, "take me into Paradise. And do Thou bless King Charles and the sweet land of France." And when he had said thus he died. And Roland looked at him as he lay. There was not upon earth a more sorrowful man than he. "Dear comrade," he said, "this is indeed an evil day. Many a year have we two been together. Never have I done wrong to you; never have you done wrong to me. How shall I bear to live without you?" And he swooned where he sat on his horse. But the stirrup held him up that he did not fall to the ground.

When Roland came to himself he looked about him and saw how great was the calamity that had befallen his army. For now there were left alive to him two only, Turpin the Archbishop and Walter of Hum. Walter had but that moment come down from the hills where he had been fighting so fiercely with the heathen that all his men were dead; now he cried to Roland for help. "Noble Count, where are you? I am Walter of Hum, and am not unworthy to be your friend. Help me therefore. For see how my spear is broken and my shield cleft in twain. My hauberk is in pieces, and my body sorely wounded. I am about to die; but I have sold my life at a great price."

When Roland heard him cry he set spurs to his horse and galloped to him. "Walter," said he, "you are a brave warrior and a trustworthy. Tell me now where are the thousand valiant men whom you took from my army. They were right good soldiers, and I am in sore need of them."

"They are dead," answered Walter; "you will see them no more. A sore battle we had with the Saracens yonder on the hills; they had the men of Canaan there and the men of Armenia and the Giants; there were no better men in their army than these. We dealt with them so that they will not boast themselves of this day's work. But it cost us dear; all the men of France lie dead on the plain, and I am wounded to the death. And now, Roland, blame me not that I fled; for you are my lord, and all my trust is in you."

"I blame you not," said Roland, "only as long as you live help me against the heathen." And as he spake he took his cloak and rent it into strips and bound up Walter's wounds therewith. This done he and Walter and the Archbishop set fiercely on the enemy. Five-and-twenty did Roland slay, and Walter slew six, and the Archbishop five. Three valiant men of war they were; fast and firm they stood one by the other; hundreds there were of the heathen, but they dared not come near to these three valiant champions of France. They stood far off, and cast at the three spears and darts and javelins and weapons of every kind. Walter of Hum was slain forthwith; and the Archbishop's armor was broken, and he wounded, and his horse slain under him.

Nevertheless he lifted himself from the ground, still keeping a good heart in his breast. "They have not overcome me yet," said he; "as long as a good soldier lives, he does not yield."

Roland took his horn once more and sounded it, for he would know whether King Charles were coming. Ah me! it was a feeble blast that he blew. But the King heard it, and he halted and listened. "My lords!" said he, "things go ill for us, I doubt not. Today we shall lose, I fear me much, my brave nephew Roland. I know by the sound of his horn that he has but a short time to live. Put your horses to their full speed, if you would come in time to help him, and let a blast be sounded by every trumpet that there is in the army." So all the trumpets in the host sounded a blast; all the valleys and hills re-echoed with the sound; sore discouraged were the heathen when they heard it.

"King Charles has come again," they cried; "we are all as dead men. When he comes he shall not find Roland alive." Then four hundred of them, the strongest and most valiant knights that were in the army of the heathen, gathered themselves into one company, and made a yet fiercer assault on Roland.

Roland saw them coming, and waited for them without fear. So long as he lived he would not yield himself to the enemy or give place to them. "Better death than flight," said he, as he mounted his good steed Veillantif, and rode towards the enemy. And by his side went Turpin the Archbishop on foot. Then said Roland to Turpin, "I am on horseback and you are on foot. But let us keep together; never will I leave you; we two will stand against these heathen dogs. They have not, I warrant, among them such a sword as Durendal."

"Good," answered the Archbishop. "Shame to the man who does not smite his hardest. And though this be our last battle, I know well that King Charles will take ample vengeance for us."

When the heathen saw these two stand together they fell back in fear and hurled at them spears and darts and javelins without number. Roland's shield they broke and his hauberk; but him they hurt not; nevertheless they did him a grievous injury, for they killed his good steed Veillantif. Thirty wounds did Veillantif receive, and he fell dead under his master. At last the Archbishop was stricken and Roland stood alone, for the heathen had fled from his presence.

When Roland saw that the Archbishop was dead, his heart was sorely troubled in him. Never did he feel a greater sorrow for comrade slain, save Oliver only. "Charles of France," he said, "come as quickly as you may! Many a gallant knight have you lost in Roncesvalles. But King Marsilas, on his part, has lost his army. For one that has fallen on this side there have fallen full forty on that." So saying he turned to the Archbishop; he crossed the dead man's hands upon his breast and said, "I commit thee to the Father's mercy. Never has man served God with a better will, never since the beginning of the world has there lived a sturdier champion of the faith. May God be good to you and give you all good things!"

Now Roland felt that his own death was near at hand. In one hand he took his horn, and in the other his good sword Durendal, and made his way the distance of a furlong or so till he came to a plain, and in the midst of the plain a little hill. On the top of the hill in the shade of two fair trees were four marble steps. There Roland fell in a swoon upon the grass. There a certain Saracen spied him. The fellow had feigned death, and had laid himself down among the slain, having covered his body and his face with blood. When he saw Roland, he raised himself from where he was lying among the slain and ran to the place, and, being full of pride and fury, seized the Count in his arms, crying aloud, "He is conquered, he is conquered, he is conquered, the famous nephew of King Charles! See, here is his sword; 'tis a noble spoil that I shall carry back with me to Arabia." Thereupon he took the sword in one hand, with the other he laid hold of Roland's beard.

But as the man laid hold, Roland came to himself, and knew that some one was taking his sword from him. He opened his eyes but not a word did he speak save this only, "Fellow, you are none of ours," and he smote him a mighty blow upon his helmet. The steel he brake through and the head beneath, and laid the man dead at his feet. "Coward," he said, "what made you so bold that you dared lay hands on Roland? Whosoever knows him will think you a fool for your deed."

And now Roland knew that death was near at hand. He raised himself and gathered all his strength together—ah me! how pale his face was!—and took in his hand his good sword Durendal. Before him was a great rock and on this in his rage and pain he smote ten mighty blows. Loud rang the steel upon the stone; but it neither brake nor splintered. "Help me," he cried, "O Mary, our Lady! O my good sword, my Durendal, what an evil lot is mine! In the day when I must part with you, my power over you is lost. Many a battle I have won with your help; and many a kingdom have I conquered, that my lord Charles possesses this day. Never has any one possessed you that would fly before another. So long as I live, you shall not be taken from me, so long have you been in the hands of a loyal knight."

Then he smote a second time with the sword, this time upon the marble steps. Loud rang the steel, but neither brake nor splintered. Then Roland began to bemoan himself. "O my good Durendal," he said, "how bright and clear thou art, shining as shines the sun! Well I mind me of the day when a voice that seemed to come from heaven bade King Charles give thee to a valiant captain; and forthwith the good King girded it on my side. Many a land have I conquered with thee for him, and now how great is my grief! Can I die and leave thee to be handled by some heathen?" And the third time he smote a rock with it. Loud rang the steel, but it brake not, bounding back as though it would rise to the sky. And when Count Roland saw that he could not break the sword, he spake again but with more content in his heart. "O Durendal," he said, "a fair sword art thou, and holy as fair. There are holy relics in thy hilt, relics of St. Peter and St. Denis and St. Basil. These heathen shall never possess thee; nor shalt thou be held but by a Christian hand."

And now Roland knew that death was very near to him. He laid himself down with his head upon the grass, putting under him his horn and his sword, with his face turned towards the heathen foe. Ask you why he did so? To show, forsooth, to

Charlemagne and the men of France that he died in the midst of victory. This done, he made a loud confession of his sins, stretching his hand to heaven, "Forgive me, Lord," he cried, "my sins, little and great, all that I have committed since the day of my birth to this hour in which I am stricken to death." So he prayed; and, as he lay, he thought of many things, of the countries which he had conquered, and of his dear fatherland France, and of his kinsfolk, and of the good King Charles. Nor, as he thought, could he keep himself from sighs and tears; yet one thing he remembered beyond all others — to pray for forgiveness of his sins. "O Lord," he said, "who art the God of truth, and didst save Daniel Thy prophet from the lions, do Thou save my soul and defend it against all perils!" So speaking he raised his right hand, with the gauntlet yet upon it, to the sky, and his head fell back upon his arm and the angels carried him to heaven. So died the great Count Roland.

The Cid

Unlike some of the other heroes told about in this book, the Cid was a real man, whose name was Rodrigo Diaz, or Ruydiez. He was born in Burgos in the eleventh century and won the name of "Cid," which means "Conqueror," by defeating five Moorish kings. This happened after Spain had been in the hands of the Arabs for more than three hundred years, so it is small wonder that the Spaniards looked upon their hero as a very remarkable man.

When Rodrigo was still a youth, his father, Diego Laynez, was grossly insulted by Don Gomez. The custom in those days was to avenge such an insult by slaying the offender; but Diego was too old and feeble to bear arms. When he finally told his son of the wrong, Rodrigo sought out Don Gomez and challenged him to fight. So bravely and skilfully did Rodrigo manage his weapons that he slew his father's enemy. Then he cut off the head and carried it to Diego.

Soon after this Diego bade his son do homage at King Ferdinand's court. Rodrigo appeared before the king, but his bearing was so defiant that Ferdinand was frightened, and banished him.

Rodrigo departed with three hundred followers, encountered some Moors, who were invading Castile, defeated them and took five of their kings captive, releasing them only after they had promised to pay tribute and to refrain from further warfare. It was these kings who first called him "Cid."

In return for his brave service Rodrigo was restored to favor and given place among the king's courtiers.

One day Dona Ximena, daughter of Don Gomez, appeared and demanded justice from the king. Recognizing Rodrigo among the courtiers, she called to him to slay her also. But both demand and cry were unheeded, for the king had been too well served by Rodrigo to listen to any accusation against him.

Three times the maiden returned with the same request, and each time she came she heard greater praise of the young hero. At last she decided to alter her demand. A fourth time she returned, consenting to forego all thoughts of vengeance if the king would order the young hero to marry her. The Cid was very willing, for he had learned to love the girl, admiring her beauty and spirit.

The marriage was celebrated with great pomp and the king gave Rodrigo four cities as a marriage portion. Rodrigo, vowing that he would not be worthy of his wife until he had won five battles, after a pious pilgrimage to the shrine of the patron saint, hastened off to Calahorra, a frontier town claimed by two kings—the kings of Castile and Oregon.

It had been decided that the dispute over the town should be settled by combat. Rodrigo became the champion of Ferdinand of Castile. The other champion, Martin Gonzalez, began, as soon as the combat opened, to taunt the Cid.

"Never again will you mount your favorite steed Babieça," he said, "never will you return to your castle; never will you see your beloved Ximena again."

But the Cid was undaunted, and had soon laid his enemy low. Great praise then was given to the Cid—so great that the knights of Castile were jealous and plotted to kill him. But the Moorish kings whom he had captured and released warned him in time to avert the danger.

Then the Cid aided Ferdinand in defeating the hostile Moors in Estremadura, after a siege of Coimbra lasting seven months.

Several other victories over his country's enemies were added to this, and then Rodrigo returned to his beloved wife.

But not for long was he permitted to remain in the quiet of home. Henry III, Emperor of Germany, complained to the Pope that King Ferdinand had refused to acknowledge his superiority. The Pope sent a message to Ferdinand, demanding homage and tribute. The demand angered both Ferdinand and the Cid.

"Never yet have we done homage," cried the Cid, "and shall we now bow to a stranger?"

A proud refusal was then sent to the Pope, and he, knowing of no better way to settle the dispute, bade Henry send a champion to meet Rodrigo. The emperor's champion was, of course, defeated, and all of Ferdinand's enemies were so awed by the outcome of the fight that none ever again demanded homage or tribute. Rodrigo was, indeed, a very useful subject. When Ferdinand died, he was succeeded by his son, Don Sancho. The latter, planning a visit to Rome, selected the Cid to accompany him. Arriving, they found that in the preparations that had been made for their reception a lower seat had been prepared for Don Sancho than for the King of France. The Cid would not suffer such a slight, and became so violent that the Pope excommunicated him. Nevertheless, the seats were made of equal height, and the Cid, who was a good Catholic, humbled himself before the Pope and was forgiven.

It was an age of great wars, and the Cid aided his king in many a brave fight. At last, in the siege of Zamora, the king was treacherously murdered, and, as he had no sons, Don Alfonso, his brother, succeeded. When he arrived at Zamora the Cid refused to acknowledge Alfonso until he should swear that he had no part in the murder. The king, angered by the Cid's attitude, plotted revenge. Opportunity came during a war with the Moors, and the Cid was banished upon a slight pretext.

"I obey, O king," replied the Cid, when he heard the decree. "I am more ready to serve you than you are to reward me. I pray that you may never more in battle need the right arm and sword that so often served your father."

Then the Cid rode away, through a crowd of weeping people, and camped outside of the city until he could make definite plans. The people longed to bring him food or offer him shelter, but they feared the displeasure of the king. One old man, however, crept outside of the city with food, declaring that he cared "not a fig" for Alfonso's commands.

The Cid needed money, and to get it he pledged two locked coffers to some Jews. The Jews in those days were much despised by the Christians, though usually very wealthy. The men, thinking that the boxes contained vast treasures, when in reality they were filled with sand, advanced the Cid 600 marks of gold. Then the hero bade farewell to his wife and children and rode away, vowing that he would return, covered with glory and carrying with him rich spoils.

Within two weeks' time the Cid and his little band of followers had captured two Moorish strongholds and carried off much spoil. The Cid then prepared a truly royal present and sent it to the king. Alfonso, upon receiving the gift, pardoned the Cid, and published an edict permitting all who wished to join in the fight against the Moors to join Rodrigo and his band.

Toledo, thanks to the valor of the Cid, soon fell into the hands of Alfonso, but a misunderstanding arose and the king insulted the Cid. The latter, in great rage, left the army and made a sudden raid on Castile. Then the Moors, knowing that the Cid had departed, took courage and captured Valencia. But the Cid, hearing of the disaster, promptly returned, recaptured the city, and sent a message to Alfonso asking for his wife and daughters. At the same time he sent more than the promised sum of money to the Jews, who up to this time had not learned that the coffers were filled with sand. To the messenger he said:

"Tell them, that although they can find nothing in the coffers but sand, they will find that the pure gold of my truth lies beneath the sand."

As the Cid was now master of Valencia, and of vast wealth, his daughters were sought in marriage by many suitors, and the marriage of both girls was celebrated with great splendor. But the Counts of Carrion, their husbands, were not brave men like the Cid, and after lingering at Valencia in idleness for two years, their weakness was clearly shown.

One evening while the Cid was sleeping, a lion broke loose from his private menagerie and entered the room where he lay. The two princes, who were playing in the room, fled, one in his haste falling into an empty vat, and the other taking refuge behind the Cid's couch. The roaring of the lion wakened the Cid, and jumping up he seized his sword, caught the lion by the mane, led it back to its cage, and calmly returned to his place.

The cowardly conduct of the Counts of Carrion roused the anger of the Cid's followers, and in the siege of Valencia that followed their conduct brought only contempt. When the Moors were finally driven away the counts asked permission to return home with their brides and gifts.

So the Cid parted from his daughters, weeping at the loss. The procession started. The first morning the counts sent their escorts ahead, and, left alone with their wives, stripped them of their garments, beat them and kicked them, and left them for dead. But Felez Muñoz, a loyal follower of the Cid's, riding back, found the two wives, bound up their wounds and obtained shelter for them in the house of a poor man whose wife and daughters promised to nurse them. Then he rode on to tell the Cid. The Cid swore that he would be avenged, and as Alfonso was responsible for the marriage, he applied to him for redress.

The king, who had long since forgiven the Cid and learned to value his services, was very angry. A battle was finally arranged. The Counts of Carrion and their uncle were defeated and banished, and the Cid returned in triumph to Valencia. Here his daughters' second marriage took place.

The Moors returned five years later, and the Cid was prepared to meet them when he received a vision of St. Peter, predicting that he would die within thirty days, but that even though dead he would triumph over his enemy. He accordingly made preparations for his death, and after appointing a successor, he gave instructions that none should weep over his death, and that his body when embalmed should be set upon his horse, Babieça, and that, with his sword Tizona in his hand, he should be led on a certain day against the enemy.

The hero died and his successor together with his wife Ximena strove to carry out his instructions. A battle was planned, and the Cid, strapped upon his war horse, rode in the van. The Moors, filled with terror, fled before him.

After the victory the body was placed in the Church of San Pedro de Cardeña, where for ten years it remained seated, in plain view of all.